UNA MARSON

SELECTED POEMS

UNA MARSON

SELECTED POEMS

EDITED BY

ALISON DONNELL

P E E P A L   T R E E

This selection
first published by Peepal Tree Press Ltd 2011
17 King's Avenue
Leeds LS6 1QS
UK

ISBN 13: 9781845231682

Supported by
ARTS COUNCIL
ENGLAND

ACKNOWLEDGEMENTS

As ever, my thanks go to the many scholars of Caribbean literature who have sustained and challenged my interests in this field. In particular, my gratitude is due to the few scholars who have shared my interest in so-called 'early' women's writing, often in the context of others' yawns and dismissals. A big cheer for Denise DeCaires Narain, Evelyn O'Callaghan, Leah Rosenberg, Honor Ford-Smith, and Giovanna Covi.

Significant acknowledgement is due to Erika Waters, whose groundbreaking early research on Una Marson's life and work laid important scholarly foundations. Her generosity is visible here in the sharing of Marson's unpublished works: 'Emergence', 'May,' 'The Seed' and 'The Joy of Mountains'. These works were recovered during her research on Una Marson conducted through grants from the Consortium on Research Training (University of the Virgin Islands), the National Endowment for the Humanities (Research Division), and Summer Bursary at Oxford (Germaine Greer, *Tulsa Studies in Women's Literature*).

I would also like to thank Professors Eddie Baugh and Mervyn Morris for their help in tracking Jamaican sources. I am indebted to my PhD student, Amorella Lamount, for her help preparing sections of this manuscript, and to my poet colleague, Peter Robinson, for his thoughtful advice on this volume.

Jeremy Poynting of Peepal Tree remains a rare blessing for those of us working in the field of Caribbean Literature. Immense gratitude is due for sending our thoughts and cherished authors into the world in such beautiful form.

My love and thanks, as always, go to Jem, Max, Asher, Charlie, George and my mother; all of whom very probably feel that Marson is the enduring absent guest at our table after twenty years of research and chatter.

CONTENTS

UNPUBLISHED c. 1944

from TOWARDS THE STARS

UNPUBLISHED LATER POEMS

INTRODUCTION

ALISON DONNELL

Una Marson was a woman of extraordinary creativity, energy and ambition, qualities which she directed towards the great causes of her time: the advancement of black women's rights and representation; the struggle against colonialism; and the strengthening of cultural and literary nationalism. Yet if her name excites interest in the early twenty-first century, then it is usually not as the Jamaican woman poet whose works pioneered the articulation of gender and racial oppression, brought Jamaican vernacular voices alongside a Wordsworthian passion for nature, and ventured to give subjectivity to powerless and marginalised subjects. If Marson is known at all, then it is often through the incomplete and even incompatible frames of female facilitator, feminine poet or feminist pioneer. She is now recognised as the originating force behind the now famous BBC Radio programme, *Caribbean Voices*, that launched the career of so many of the Caribbean's 'great' male literary figures, and sometimes noted as having acted as a secretary to HIM Haile Selassie shortly after Mussolini's invasion of Abyssinia in 1935. The irony of her historical framing as a female facilitator to male repute can be gleaned by fuller attention to both her life and her written works. Marson is an ardent and audacious articulator of women's experiences and perspectives but the retrospective label of 'first Caribbean feminist poet' is also one that unduly constrains the scope of her value and influence.

In selecting poems by Una Marson for this first collection of her poems that provides an adequate range of her work, the imperative of representation takes on a particular charge. Marson has been both feted and forgotten, championed and censored. Her works, both poetic and activist, have been repeatedly sampled to cast her as feminist or feminine; as nationalist or internationalist; as traditionalist or experimenter. Represented in different historical moments in such a way that significant parts of her archive have been allowed to masquerade as the whole, Marson remains a tricky figure to recover. Yet, while her sidelining within both literary and cultural histories is clearly lamentable, it is not incomprehensible. She rests on the margins of a Caribbean literary tradition, not only because her work is very diverse, even seemingly contradictory, but because many of her writings are still dismissed as unyielding and unrewarding, even un-Caribbean. In particular, the elements of mimicry and pastiche in her works, along with her excessively devotional love poetry, and her use of orthodox poetic forms and archaic language continue to elicit embarrassed critical silences. The mixed bag of devotional sonnets, love lyrics, feminist parodies, Afro-blues and folk monologues that comprise her four volumes of poetry struggle to be identified with the clean, sharp edges of male nationalist writings that dominate the political project of Caribbean writing in the 1930s, although her work bears interesting comparison to that of the Jamaican poet George Campbell. Similarly, her complicated and intricate tracing of female desire and the gendered constraints of women's lives put pressure on the neat frames of feminist criticism, that have sought to reclaim her as a lost foremother. Even her rendering of creole voices sits awkwardly alongside her continued fascination with hyperbole and her precarious play with clichéd high poetic diction.

   This collection of Marson's poems consciously rejects the categorizing of her work according to oppositional poetic and political modes: either sentimental or polemical, feminine or feminist, resistant or complicit. Rather, the poems selected here aim to set these seemingly competing archives of her work alongside each other in order to foreground and to invest positively in what might be seen as Marson's poetic unevenness. The striking range of both poetic content and register that characterises her work invites readers to confront the cultural volatility of 'early' postcolonial writings, as well

12

as the kinds of critical guarantees that are often looked for under the rubrics of agency and liberation. The inclusivity of this collection is not only a matter of historical record but also a recognition of how historical processes shape both acts of writing and its reception. Demonstrating the full range of Marson's works is significant because it enables an appreciation of her development as a poet and affords a strong sense of how different social contexts and historical moments impacted profoundly upon her cultural and political sensibilities, as well as the kinds of linguistic and formal resources that she chose to draw upon.

In a few instances, where consistency supported it, I made small corrections to the punctuation and grammar.

Publishing History

Marson published three volumes of poetry during the 1930s: *Tropic Reveries* in 1930, *Heights and Depths* in 1931, and *The Moth and The Star* in 1937. All of these volumes were self-published and printed by The Gleaner Co. Ltd. in Kingston, Jamaica. In the preface to *Tropic Reveries*, Marson notes that some of the poems included in this volume had been published in *The Cosmopolitan* magazine, which she edited, and in other local newspapers. These were published in the late 1920s and appear to mark the start of her career as a published poet.

Tropic Reveries presents sixty poems, divided into 'Lyrics', 'Sonnets' and 'Miscellaneous Poems'. The short author's preface describes her poetry as, ' "heart-throbs" of one who from the earliest childhood has worshipped at the shrine of the muses and dwelt among the open spaces and the silent hills where the cadences of Nature's voice tempt one to answering song' (p. v). It is certainly true that the volume is densely populated with romantic and pastoral scenes and displays little evidence of technical talent or poetic innovation. However, the fact that it is formally tame does not prohibit the stirrings of a politically adventurous voice. The volume accommodates a sonnet sequence staging self-sacrificial love as well as two bold canonical parodies on the state of marriage, suggesting that her serrated sensibility in relation to gender as a social script was already formed.

Heights and Depths published just one year later, continues to devote poetic attention to romantic love and the natural world, with the seventy-one poems now arranged under 'Poems of Nature', 'Poems of Love' and 'Miscellaneous Poems'. The formal dimensions of this volume are also overwhelmingly drawn from canonical English works but there are brief glimmers of the declarative voice that will so strongly inform the intense and urgent works written during and after her time in England. Both 'Another Mould' and 'There Will Come A Time', take their energy from a stand against injustice and discrimination.

It is unquestionably in *The Moth and The Star* that Marson's poetic voice finds its most subtle, daring and influential form. Her works are here arranged under 'Poems Written in England', 'Poems of Nature', 'Poems of Love' and 'Poems of Life'. Unsurprisingly, given her time spent in England and her involvement with women's organisations and 'race associations', the poems which appear in this third volume are far more directly engaged with the politics of difference, and are concerned with giving subjectivity and direct voice to Jamaican people, as well as with representing the interwoven negative pressures confronting the black female subject. While it is Marson's works on these subjects, all of which are collected here, that have attracted most critical attention in the last two decades, it remains important to acknowledge that there are still thirty-one love poems in this volume. Possibly because she was physically remote from the natural world of Jamaica in the years leading up to its publication, there are only thirteen nature poems and often the pastoral vision is inflected by a consciousness of class, as in 'Heartbreak Cottages' and of power, as in 'Winged Ants'.

In 1945, the University of London Press Ltd published a fourth and final volume, *Towards the Stars*, with approximately half the publication reprinted from earlier works. The ordering of her works here follows the structure of *The Moth and The Star*, on which she draws heavily. There is some evidence of textual editing, as many of the poems have different punctuation. In just a few instances, there are more substantial revisions, such as 'At The Prison Gates' which now carries the subtitle, 'Jamaica, 1937', which points more directly to its rendering of an actual historical event. 'The Stone Breakers' and 'My Philosophy' both carry a note to indicate that they are 'Written in Jamaican dialect'. Although only a handful of significant revisions occur, they would seem to suggest that Marson, aided by her English friend and fellow writer, Stella Mead, was aware of the need for some cultural mediation in order to present her poems to an English audience.

As something resembling a collected works, this volume offers us insight into how Marson valued her own poetry and how she chose to frame it for an English audience. From a total of sixty-four poems, thirty-five are taken from *The Moth and The Star*. Only one poem, 'There will come a time…', appears from the 1931 collection, *Heights and Depths* and none from the 1930 *Tropic Reveries*. Yet, while Marson's preference for her later poems may be clear in this volume, her selection and organisation of material does not straightforwardly support a claim for the foregrounding of more explicitly politicised works. The volume opens with fifteen 'Nature poems', continues with twenty-three 'Love poems' and concludes with twenty-six 'Poems of Life'. Critics and readers would now attach greater weight and value to the poems that appear in this final section, including her works rendering the vernacular voices of Jamaican 'folk', those against racism such as 'Black Burden' and 'Little Brown Girl', and her poems in praise of women's strength and solidarity, such as 'To the I.A.W.S.E.C.' and 'Winifred Holtby'. All the same, despite Marson's unequivocal politicisation during the 1930s, a process that occurred both through her encounter with the realities of racism in Britain and her involvement with the national struggle in Jamaica during the turbulent end to that decade, her own framing of the poetic works and identity remain consistent. In each of her volumes, Nature and Love poetry are presented first and although the 'Miscellaneous' poems of *Heights and Depths* become the more assertive and promi-nent 'Poems of Life' in the last two volumes, these still appear as the final section.

Although the arrangement of poems within these volumes does

not have any bearing on the critical availability of Marson's work, what is important here is that the temptation to read her poetry as developing a more politicised profile – though valid in many ways, as well as being in tune with contemporary critical sensibilities – needs to be tempered by the recognition that in her own terms, her poetry was never directed only at the struggles against racial prejudice and towards women's empowerment. Interesting in this regard is the exclusion from her own selected volume of 'Cinema Eyes' and 'Kinky Hair Blues' that arguably articulate her most significant and enduring achievement. These poems, along with others, represent the entanglements of race and gender as sites of both oppression and division but they also render for black womanhood an identity of beauty, empowerment and solidarity. The fact that these poems are not selected may indicate that Marson was keen to court a conservative postwar English audience, but it may also be a consequence of the fact that she had not received recognition for these works in the eight years since their publication.

While it is difficult to trace anything more than glimpses of critical opinion relating to Marson's work during this period, it is evident from the few poems of hers that are anthologised in the 1940s and 50s that a more conservative and traditional profile was still in circulation. *A Treasury of Jamaican Poetry* edited by J. E. Clare McFarlane and published by the University of London Press in 1949 includes 'Darlingford' and 'The Approach', firmly framing Marson as a nature poet. Perhaps most intriguing for us as contemporary readers is the selection of two poems by Marson in *The Poetry Of The Negro 1746-1949*, edited by Langston Hughes and Arna Bontemps, also published in 1949. Neither address the anthology's stated theme of 'the Negro's experience in the Western world' (preface vii), unlike several of Marson's other poems which provide a direct and compelling perspective on this experience. 'Hunted' (not collected here) and 'Nightfall', are both rather plaintive and dramatic short pieces that characteristically smudge the pain of lost love with the emotional consolation offered by the natural world. Interestingly, 'Nightfall' was also the single poem to appear in *The Anthology of Poetry of the West Indies* (unpublished 1953), chosen and edited by W. Adolphe Roberts and Wycliffe Bennett. The *Kyk-Over-Al*

1952 Anthology of West Indian Poetry included three of Marson's poems, all new works from *Towards the Stars*: 'The Impossible', 'Conspiracy' and 'Where Death was Kind'. These poems, all of which touch on the subject of lost love, may confirm that Marson's work 'has a simplicity and dignity', as L. A. G. Strong, a writer whom Marson had met through her BBC work, comments in his introduction to the volume. Yet, again, none of these poems, nor others that were anthologised, register the political sensibilities that informed her later works nor the daring, even defiant, language of racial abuse that she also insisted on writing into poetic form.

Critical Reception

These indications of how Marson's work circulated within her lifetime are too thin to draw firm conclusions from, yet they do suggest a fairly consistent profiling of her as a poet who wrote with a passion about lost love and with an elegance about the natural world. Similar and enduring acts of profiling also emerge from the glimpses of critical response that do exist. In his introduction to *Heights and Depths*, Sir William Morrison expresses his belief that the poems in the volume are 'strongly indicative of the poetic temperament of its Author', laying down the biographical-literary line of analysis that has proved particularly tenacious. Morrison praises Marson's preference for Jamaica as poetic subject and also draws attention to works that represent 'women's problems'.

Introducing *The Moth and the Star* in 1937, Philip M. Sherlock, the founding father of the University of the West Indies, but also a white Jamaican and Knight of the British Empire, identifies the nationalistic feeling with which Marson's poems are imbued. Although he condones 'Miss Marson's love of her homeland and its people' (p. xii), Sherlock suggests that her emotional utterance tends towards the excessive in other works, displaying 'more of sentimentality than of sentiment' (xii). While he evaluates Marson's poems addressing issues of racial politics as 'hectic and forced' (p. xi), he praises those poems in which he senses a 'note of quiet assurance' of racial identity. Intriguingly, Sherlock reads Marson's blues poems as statements of authenticity rather than protest, and esteems these, along with her 'dialect' works, as her greatest achievements, asserting that she 'has captured the spirit of the people' (p. x).

L. A. G. Strong's introduction to *Towards the Stars* in 1945 continues the appraisal of Marson's poetry as autobiographical: 'the personality revealed in the letter… was manifest also in the poems' (p. 3). Strong, a writer met at the BBC, struggles to find a way to connect productively with her style and gestures clumsily towards a 'negro' in *Porgy* who hammers on a box in order to express the spontaneous quality he identifies in his work. His naive deficiency in summoning a critical vocabulary capable of articulating the complex range of poetic subjects and styles that comprise her poetry make visible the absence of any meaningful correspondence between Marson's intensely-felt understanding of race and that of her English middle-class audience.

As a Jamaican man of letters, J. E. Clare McFarlane's 1957 book, *A Literature in the Making*, which chronicled the leading figures of the Poetry League of Jamaica during the 1930s and 1940s, has a short chapter on Marson's work. He focuses Marson's poetic achievements on her 'dialect' poems: 'her revival of interest in the thought and sentiment of the common people as expressed through the medium created by themselves' (p. 96). This is an interesting shift given his decision to anthologise such linguistically conventional poems in his 1949 volume. However, it would be misleading to suggest a clear or progressive line in the understanding of her poetic value. In his 1956 article, 'The Literary Situation in the Caribbean', Henry Swanzy, the producer of the BBC *Caribbean Voices* Programme that Marson had helped to found, argued that 'the personal life has been explored by the poetess Una Marson in a collection *Towards the Stars*'. Indeed, as late as 1979, Reinhard Sander's essay in Bruce King's *West Indian Literature* only offers tepid praise for what is considered to be a 'mildly' enlightened poetic stance: 'though dependent on borrowed tradition, [it] begins to show an awareness of contemporary poetic techniques and attitudes' (p.59).

One noteworthy trend in these early critical responses is that even those critics alert to the progressiveness of Marson's poetic voice in terms of cultural politics and the imperatives of cultural nationalism fail to appreciate her equally powerful and innovative exploration of gender identity. Indeed, critical recognition of her works that voiced the particularities of women's lives, whether in sincere, humorous or indignant register, did not appear until almost half a century after the publication of Marson's four volumes. All the same, it was this belated acknowledgement of her ground-breaking status as a black woman poet that was crucial to the revival of her literary reputation. Indeed, it is no coincidence that 'Kinky Hair Blues' and 'To Wed or Not To Wed' are now her most anthologised works.

In his *West Indian Poetry* (1978), Lloyd Brown claims Marson as 'the earliest female poet of significance to emerge in West Indian literature' (p. 34). He also foregrounds the importance of gender as a poetic trope and identifies the link between her experience of England and her awareness of racial oppression: 'exile to a predomi-nantly white society sharpens her ethnic perceptions' (p. 34). Nevertheless, Brown dismisses *Tropic Reveries* as 'extremely immature ... adolescent love lyrics'. His tending to discuss gender only as awareness of oppression, a position motivated by the political claims being made for women's literature and black writing during the 1970s and 1980s, leaves unexamined the complex representation of gendered consciousness offered by her work as a whole.

Also in the 1980s, critical essays devoted solely to her poetry began to appear and the voice of the female literary critic was heard. Erika Smilowitz's biographical article 'Una Marson – A Woman Before Her Time', in 1983, and her critical reading, ' "Weary of Life and All My Heart's Dull Pain": The Poetry of Una Marson', in 1984, powerfully recover the significance of gender within Marson's poetry. Smilowitz declares that she 'wrote as a woman. Her poems tell of passion, of desire, of frustrated love and above all, of loneliness' (p. 63). Moreover, her much-needed research into Marson's life and writ-ings structured an intense connectivity between the two bodies of knowledge that tended to privilege Marson's poetic rendering of vulnerability and loss. For Smilowitz, 'Marson leaves no doubt in her reader's mind as to her perception of the plight of women, and it is a convincingly despondent picture' (p. 24).

A similar resolve upon a stable gendered identity appears in Honor Ford Smith's article, 'Una Marson: Black Nationalist and Feminist Writer', also from the mid 1980s. Again, the matrix of experience and cultural expression organises a defining framework for literary evaluation. Ford Smith's paper is a landmark piece in its contextualizing of Marson's work within women's organizations and 'race associations' of her time, but her analysis of Marson's poetry is swayed by the tug of these political affiliations. Unlike Smilowitz, Ford-Smith does not focus on the first two volumes but rather foregrounds the elements of ideological resistance in *The Moth and The Star*.

Drawing on two very different archives, these almost opposing versions of Marson as woman poet can be sustained. Yet constructing her poetic reputation according to these selective possibilities is to deny the critical rewards and political challenges of seeking to negotiate the seemingly irreconcilable and competing versions of woman, poet and black subject that her writings set in motion. During the 1990s, Marson's name flickered among the pages of black British histories and now features on many web pages devoted to this subject. She commonly figures fleetingly in these narratives and usually as a forgotten foremother, an early feminist and a 'first woman' publisher, broadcaster, speaker.

While it may be tempting to recover Marson as a less ambiguous poet in order to secure her reputation within the fields of women's writing and Caribbean poetry, to read her as somehow fully feminine or feminist is to misrepresent her work and prevent future substantive readings. As Denise DeCaires Narain has persuasively argued, 'her reputation need not rest so exclusively on those poems in which she handles themes that are explicitly concerned with black women's realities' (DeCaires Narain 2002, p. 46). Marson was a complex figure and, just as it would be disingenuous to mention only her triumphs and achievements as a writer and social and political campaigner when it is well-known that she suffered from clinical depression and was often unfulfilled and lonely, so too it would be misleading to suggest that Marson wrote only strident, progressive poetry. Very many of her poems are about frustrations in love and the solace and fortitude that the natural world can offer. Indeed, rather than view the volatility of her work as a problem to be critically resolved or erased, her poetry can be seen as a fascinating if unsettling archive that makes visible the contradictions and tensions of the dramatic history through which she lived.

Life

It is certainly true that reading many of the anthologising projects of Jamaican poetry during the first half of the twentieth century, which sometimes present a too detached and stable collection of nature and love poetry, it would be possible to conclude that this poetry removed itself from history. In some respects this detachment was wilfully attained and many of the writers who chose poetry seemed mainly to perceive it as a vehicle for the communication of conservative spiritual and aesthetic values. Indeed, poetry in Jamaica in the 1930s appears to have been favoured by those striving to achieve the communication of so-called 'universal' values, above and beyond local concerns. In this respect, poetry's general relation to history was dramatically different from that of much prose written at this time which was actively inscribing the realities of everyday experience, particularly of yard and barrack room life, in a conscious attempt to centre the literary on Jamaican realities. As a key figure in Jamaican poetry circles, J. E. C. McFarlane probably spoke influentially on 'The Challenge of Our Time' when he addressed the Poetry League of Jamaica in 1935: 'Therefore as representatives of a great tradition we offer you Poetry, upon which we feel certain the true foundation of this Empire rests and by which it will be preserved throughout the storm that hangs above the horizon of civilization' (p. 29).

Marson, however, although earlier involved with the Poetry League of Jamaica, was not a poet or a person removed from history. The publication of Delia Jarrett-Macauley's *The Life of Una Marson, 1905-1965* in 1998 has been central to a fuller appreciation of both the intricate emotional and impassioned political navigations that Marson sought to make during her lifetime. Indeed, her life may be read as a conscious attempt to follow C.L.R. James's edict for West Indians to 'write ourselves into history'. Her work consistently reflects her strong sense of herself and other Jamaicans as historical subjects charged with a responsibility to broker new terms for their future. Marson's poetic career coincided with a period of immense cultural and political upheaval in Jamaica and the Caribbean more widely, and she had a strong sense of a moment of change within her lifetime that was to be captured and activated. The 1930s is commonly identified as the defining decade for the formation of national consciousness and a new political imaginary that broke the loyalty to Empire. While the formation of trade unions and political parties offers an obvious indicator of such change, the role of cultural activism and the rise of print cultures should not be underestimated in terms of allowing new ideas of civil society and committed cultural communities to come into view.

Marson's own little magazine project, *The Cosmopolitan: A Monthly Magazine for the Business Youth of Jamaica and the Official Organ of the Stenographers Association*, was first published in May 1928. It was the first Jamaican periodical to have a woman editor-publisher and its gender politics were explicit, with an editorial statement proclaiming: 'This is the age of woman: what man has done, women may do.' Although torn between the demands of her audience for news on fashion and tips on housekeeping, and her commitment to induct Jamaica's growing body of working women into contemporary political debates, the magazine become an important outlet for Marson's views on industrial change, gender and national politics, as well as a regular space for the publication of local writing, with a page dedicated to 'Short Poems by Local Poets'. It is clear that her aim was to reconcile the interests of Jamaicans, particularly young professional women, to the ideals of equality and inclusivity, as well as to the interests of the world beyond their island home.

The magazine's editorial statement from May 1930 reveals Marson advocating the need to loosen up a cosy, middle-class nationalism that affirmed prosperity, and wanting to ruffle a demure femininity as the norm of female existence. She invoked cosmopolitanism as a way of being open to the world, both near and far, and was critical of those Jamaicans blind to the lives of the majority population with whom they had daily contact but whom they did not properly recognize as co-citizens: 'We have endeavoured to foster a 'COSMO-

POLITAN' spirit, a wider vision, a more charitable and tolerant attitude among all sections of our small society. We abhor narrowness, snobbishness and such things which do more to engender strife and unhappiness than all the other causes put together… we must build up a clean, thoughtful and artistic Island literature' (*Cosmopolitan* May 1930, p. 5). From the very start of her publishing career, social justice and cultural transformation were linked ideas. Marson's intellectual energy was never abstracted from her reading of a world in need of change, and it is easy to trace her determination to see her ideas translated into action. She did not pursue the conventional avenues to personal recognition but consistently sought to initiate and participate in collective action, as well as to affirm her religious conviction as a source of unity.

After a flurry of writing activity with the publication of her first two poetry volumes in 1930 and 1931 and the staging, to public acclaim, of her first play, *At What a Price*, in Kingston at the Ward Theatre, Marson left for England, arriving in Plymouth on 9 July 1932. Although Marson's arrival in London coincided historically with that of C.L.R. James, her cultural and intellectual ideas set her apart from the West Indian 'angry young men' who came in the 1930s. Marson lodged at the home of a fellow Jamaican, Dr Ronald Moody, in Peckham, and soon became involved with the League of Coloured Peoples, an organization that Moody had founded in 1931 to address the issues of racial division and prejudice. As editor of the League's journal, *The Keys*, Marson was easily networked into black British and West Indian circles and had opportunities to meet many of the key figures in the emergent nationalist and anti-colonial movements. Her interest in pan-Africanism developed during this period, fostered by her close association with Sir Nana Ofori Atta, an African king from northern Ghana, whom Marson met in 1934 when he headed a delegation from the Gold Coast to the Colonial Office.

We know from *The Cosmopolitan* that Marson's own priorities for a feminist agenda – awareness of inequality, responsibility to others, collaboration, and public action – were already in place before this first visit to London. All the same, her interest in women's rights developed vigorously and in 1934 she gave a speech at the Women's

23

International League Conference in London. In 1935 her interna-
tionalism and conviction on issues of women's rights meant that she
was the first Jamaican and first woman of African descent invited to
speak at the International Alliance of Women for Suffrage and Equal
Citizenship Conference in Istanbul and, in the same year, the first
black woman invited to attend the League of Nations at Geneva. Here
a meeting with the Abyssinian delegation at the conference further
raised her awareness of the urgent struggle against colonialism. Her
time spent in Britain offered Marson an enabling context within
which to develop her ideas on black unity and women's rights. As
Anna Snaith has observed, 'While Marson often felt marginalized in
the capital, her work took her inside the very institutions and
organizations that upheld notions of Britishness and empire, such as
the Colonial office, the BBC and the British Commonwealth League'
(Snaith, 2008, p. 110). Both her poetry written during this period
and her journalism published in Jamaica, most notably a cluster of
articles published in *Public Opinion* in 1937, reveal the painful
dimensions of living in a white majority society in which ideas of
entitlements and expressions of self were compromised by embed-
ded attitudes towards race. Although Marson's poetry as a whole
reveals the way in which ideas of identity, culture and power are
constantly being re-examined, her entry into the social context of
England offers the clearest shift. While there is a distinctive and
somewhat orthodox idea of poetic authority and subject that informs
her first two volumes, the political voice that is directed towards
journalism in Jamaica is distilled into a much more textured and
intensely observed poetic medium during and after her encounter
with England.

Significantly, from 1932 onwards all of her writings show an
awareness of the way in which political identities are shaped by race,
as if, as Fanon describes it, 'the first encounter with a white man
oppresses him with the whole weight of his blackness' (*Black Skin
White Masks*, p. 150). The politics of solidarity that she had advocated
between different social groups in Jamaica is clearly differently
loaded by her life in Britain, most significantly in the direction of
black unity. The idea of woman, which she draws on as a relatively
stable category in Jamaica, always with attention to class difference

but also in anticipation of gender solidarity, is no longer realizable. In an undated manuscript, 'Problems of Coloured People in Britain', she begins:

> The young coloured woman has to face many problems. More often than not she is poorly educated and she finds the problem of finding work a serious one... In London, most avenues of work except that of entertaining in the dance or Music halls, are closed to coloured people... I know of their difficulties and I myself have experienced difficulty in finding work when I urgently needed it. Once I tried to register for work as a stenographer. One agent told me she didn't register black women because they would have to work in offices with white women. Another agent tried to find me a position and he told me that though my references were excellent firms did not want to employ a black stenographer. (No date, Una Marson Papers box 1944C, 1)

Her poems of this period also reflect the hostile social context of England, and an acute sense of alienation. As her own urgency for paid work indicates, Marson's economic insecurity compounded her sense of being on the outside of English society and her poems show an alertness to class divisions. Her poetic rendering of the lowly privates in 'They Also Serve', the labourers in the makeshift, impermanent dwellings of 'Heartbreak Cottages' show her sensitivity to the different lives of English people, just as she was aware of the diverse fortunes of the labouring and market women in Jamaica from those of the middle-classes. Indeed, it is a striking measure of the sting of racial prejudice that Marson deploys the term 'urchins' pejoratively in her 1933 poem 'Nigger'. The indignation at the cruelty and power shown by these poor children's racial abuse provokes another form of stereotyping, demonstrating the difficulties of forming a consistent politics of equality in an environment layered with class and race-based conflicts and tensions. Although Marson's four year spell in Britain was clearly informative and transformative, it was not always emotionally fulfilling. Provoked and outraged by Mussolini's invasion of Abyssinia in 1935, Marson immediately offered her help to Dr. Martin, the Ethiopian Minister. She went on to provide secretarial support to HIM Haile Selassie, but by September of 1936 she was severely depressed and returned to Jamaica.

Her return coincided with the pinnacle period of cultural and political upheaval in Jamaica and the Caribbean more widely. The 1930s was a time of economic depression and, in the West Indies, poor social conditions, low wages and high infant mortality made the life of most colonial subjects insufferable. The Wall Street Crash of 1929 impacted on the Caribbean but the local crash in crop prices and workers wages, along with the end of economic migration to the Canal Zone, caused severe local distress and turmoil. Increasingly intense social and political unrest became evident as a wave of riots and strikes moved across the West Indies, with labour rebellions in Barbados, British Guiana and Jamaica, as well as Trinidad. It was in Jamaica in 1938 that the conflict between colonial law and workers' power came to a head with the dock workers strike, but before this it was evident that demands for representation and self-government were gaining ground. While Marson had been in England, the climate of political ferment and the promise of defining change in terms of political understandings had clearly inspired her own vision of what might be possible for Jamaicans, and women and the working-classes, once the stranglehold of Empire had been broken.

Being back home in Jamaica seems to have restored Marson's public voice and her commitment to politics. She soon founded Jamaica's Readers and Writers Club and wrote a regular, and often fiercely political column in *Public Opinion*, the weekly paper of the People's National Party led by Norman Manley. It was also in September of 1937 that Marson published her third volume of poetry, *The Moth and the Star*, and her third play, *Pocomania*, was staged in January 1938 at the Ward Theatre, Kingston. Retaining her early practical commitment to social justice, Marson worked hard to raise money for a Jamaica Save the Children Association while also reporting for the *Jamaican Standard*. Yet despite such a whirl of publicly engaged activity, in 1938 Marson returned to London in order to report on, and to, the Moyne Commission (a British

Government initiative investigating the riots and unrest that had swept across the Caribbean region) and to fund-raise for Jamsave.

After the declaration of war in 1939, she wrote about changes in the black community in Britain, as fewer students made the journey and many of those based in London moved North. Marson's own fortunes improved when she took freelance work with the BBC and in 1941 was appointed full-time assistant for the radio programme *Calling the West Indies* that had developed, by 1945, into the now famous *Caribbean Voices* literary showcase. She was in fragile health when *Towards the Stars* was published just before her return to Jamaica. It is a mark of her prominence at that time that she was met by huge crowds and a lunch was organized in her honour by the Poetry League of Jamaica. Marson worked for some years for the nationalist Pioneer Press, the book publishing arm of the *Gleaner*.

Work

The literary quest for an appropriate voice and form during a time of such linguistic and cultural flux was both testing and insistent for Caribbean poets. The persistent, almost subterranean, influence of a colonial education and the enduring cultural prestige attributed to canonical writers and writings were not to be easily dismissed. The tropes and forms of canonical English Literature leave distinct traces within Marson's work but they do not necessarily constrain her more traditionally poetic works and often these are neither static nor inert in their politics. Indeed, Marson's poetic writings energetically address the challenge of finding a literary voice for her own time and place from many directions. How to write as a woman? How to write as a black subject, a modern subject, a diasporic subject? How to write for the poor and powerless?

My aim in this collection is to make these very different, some-times contradictory, 'voicings' within Marson's poetry both visible and intelligible. Gathering together a diverse set of poems, across the three volumes, casts her poetry as a fascinating expressive archive for the writing in of identity differences and complicated structures of feeling that, by turn, both unsettle and reassure our sense of how these emergent subjectivities may take shape. All the same, there are a number of themes that continue to inform her work across the four collections, as well as some striking departures and developments in terms of both form and content, particularly within *The Moth and The Star*. While I would suggest that a pathless ramble across the patchy terrain of Marson's poetry may offer its own rewards, I also recognise that a few signposts and points of interest may be helpful tools in navigating a productive journey.

Poems of Nature

All of Marson's poetry volumes contain a significant number of Nature poems. In many ways, her relationship to the natural world would seem to provide the most immediate and inspiring material for her poetry. In the twenty-first century age of eco-criticism when nature is regarded as a source of deep and intimate local knowledge and landscape offers a privileged relation to a sensibility of belonging, the connection between expressive culture and the natural environment is seen as direct and authentic. While some of Marson's nature poetry seeks exactly this kind of relationship to nature, the strain and complication of her relationship to the physical realities of her world, always already mediated through the colonial archive, must also be recognised. Yet, her reliance on a Romantic vision should not be seen as a particular failing but rather as symptomatic of a generation for whom, as the novelist Vic Reid argued, 'culturally, our concern was with Keats; our fascination was with the View from Westminster Bridge. Even those two best among our political and social awakeners, N. W. Manley and his cousin Alexander Bustamante, were not immune to matters of King and Empire. Jamaica was a cultural wasteland that exiled sanity... But a sense of renewal was surging against those bonds of remembered bondage' (Reid, p. 3). Both the lack of confidence in Jamaica as its own world and the increasing resistance to its denial as a distinctive and cherished landscape can be traced in Marson's nature poetry. Although there is a sincere investment in the beauty and joy of nature, in poems such as 'The Meeting of The Clouds' and 'The Speedwell', the simple solace of nature that is celebrated in 'Nature's Heart', is woven into a matrix of romantic and spiritual affiliations, as if the natural world becomes a mode of reflection rather than a physical reality.

In those Nature poems that appear in *The Moth and The Star*, the praise for natural beauty and criticism of the devaluation of human life are more explicitly related. In 'To the Hibiscus', which combines the gesture of naming the landscape with an implicit allegory of historical injustice, the fragile flower stands for the Jamaican people, who have experienced the physical and psychological damage of imperialism, and, like them, it holds the promise of flourishing through liberty. The flower then becomes a poetic emblem of justice and, despite romanticising the poor, this poem, like 'Vagabond Creed' does address social inequality and the need to map more than the aesthetics of the natural world.

Poems for Jamaica

Although they often celebrate the natural world, Marson's poems written for Jamaica offer a heightened example of the kinds of aesthetic and political problems that she had to negotiate as a poet working within and against the accepted poetic register of her place and time. These poems are ripe with internal contradictions and make visible the ways in which the literary quest to represent an 'authentic' Jamaica was already compromised and entangled by the prestige models of colonial literary landscapes that created the constant recourse to culture, even for representations of Nature. While 'Darlingford' invests positively in the beauty and awe of a Jamaican landscape and contributes to the naming and claiming of a distinct and local geography that brings forward ideas of national belonging, the other poems collected here are more conflicted.

The troubled allusion to an Edenic vision first appears in *Tropic Reveries* in 'Jamaica', with the Jamaican landscape framed as a positive inversion of an English scene. A vision of natural opulence which balances on the very edge of stereotype, also appears in 'Jamaica' of *Heights And Depths*. However, 'In Jamaica', in the same volume, offers a self-conscious representation of Jamaica as a prelapsarian world. The explicit references to the divide which exists between tourists and slum dwellers, and between black and white Jamaicans, reveals the image and experience of Jamaica as a toil-free, exotic island to be dependent upon the very material realities of its social and ethnic hierarchies. In 'Heartbreak Cottages', the representation of the homes of the poor foregrounds those elements of the Jamaican landscape which cannot be accommodated within an Edenic vision. As in other works, Marson here appeals to nature's beauty in order to point to the unequal social geography of the island and to issue a demand for change and an appeal to national inclusivity.

An awareness of the way in which the Jamaica of Jamaicans is always already culturally mediated surfaces in 'Home Thoughts', written in England and published in *The Moth and the Star*. Like 'Nostalgia', this rendering of Jamaica from the vantage point of England is fraught with ambiguity, and at times both poems move towards the earlier 'paradise' vision. 'Home Thoughts' is interesting in its admission of the poetic pull towards the description of an English landscape and the representation of Jamaica in this poem is certainly a site of complex cultural affiliations and overlapping discourses.

Poems of Love

In the context of Jamaican colonial culture, in which acquiescence, mimicry and subordination were everyday imperatives, the presentations of willing devotion and female dependence which dominate Marson's love poems are understandably difficult to interpret. It is perhaps not surprising that in their assumed demonstration of emotional and literary immaturity and excitability, Marson's love poems represent the neglected archive of an already marginalized poet. Both their content and form present a problem to feminist and postcolonial critical approaches that commonly work in parallel to foreground moments of agency and resistance. Although these poems bring forward an alertness to the fact that Marson's more recent recovery, thanks mainly to the burgeoning of black feminist criticism of the 1980s onwards, often entails a forgetting of her many love lyrics, the inclusion of these works here is not only strategic.

The selection of love poetry, made across her first three volumes, aims to show the creative space that Marson crafts for woman in her structuring of romance, devotion and emotional excess. The overlapping of romance and mastery that is a repeated refrain in her love poems creates a troubling matrix of signs, and yet the recurring image of the woman achieving self-definition through the act of giving the self disrupts a simplistic reading of devotion to either the lover figure or to eurocentric poetic forms. In addition, the way in which women's desire is constantly positioned at an oblique angle to the figure of the lover also opens up interesting questions about the assured containment of female emotions within the paradigm of heterosexual romance.

Most significant in this regard are the ten sonnets, from 'Renunciation' to 'Absence', that follow the plot of the romantic quest from the need and desire for love, into the pulls and pushes of expectation and fulfilment, and beyond the encounter with the lover, and therefore beyond the conventional consummation, into an aestheticized indulgence of the lover as a creative ideal. The almost systematic navigation of an affair of the heart offered by these sonnets from *Tropic Reveries* provides an early and influential template for her later love poems. In 'Resignation' from *Heights and Depths* the reluctance to consummate and the actual relationship to the lover as a painful and trifling affair continues. Both 'I Care Not' from *Heights and Depths* and 'The Heart's Cunning' from *The Moth and The Star* maintain the discourse of indulgent martyrdom. When read carefully and collectively, poems such as 'The Impossible', 'Reasoning', 'Love Songs' and 'My Beloved' can be seen to deflect the charges of dependency and sentimentality that they may initially invite by consistently sculpting the lover as a poetic creation or abstraction, enjoyed and cherished most fully when absent. There is also an expression of erotic need, in 'Resignation', that is surprising and daring.

This collection seeks to represent the impressive range of political causes that Marson was engaged in, as well as her remarkable appreciation of the need for an integrated political sensibility which brought the struggles and conceptions of social justice relating to race, gender and class into each other's orbits. Nevertheless, it is important to recognise that her status as a woman poet who writes consciously of gender has been absolutely fundamental to Marson's critical recuperation. Reading these poems that render the realities of women's lives and the particular difficulties and demands that women face within a culture organised around eurocentric and patriarchal norms alongside her love poetry is to listen to a poetic voice being pulled in many directions and to witness the competing versions of female fulfilment that jostled for position within her cultural worlds.

Marson's parodies, 'To Wed or Not to Wed' and 'If', offer a clear intervention in terms of the gendering of literary and experiential authority. Trespassing within the formal territory of the English masters, Shakespeare and Kipling, these poems not only critique the institution of marriage but also the cultural expectation that the problems and decisions men must confront are innately more serious and significant than those facing women. The initial humour of 'To Wed or Not to Wed' exists in its mock-heroic subject matter and the comic comparison between Hamlet, the intellectual hero and 'sweet prince', and the undistinguished, single female. However, given the historical context of Jamaica and the moral pressure exerted on women to marry and thus gain respectability, it may not be extravagant to compare 'The fret and loneliness of spinsterhood' to Hamlet's 'sea of troubles'.

The parody of Kipling's 'If', the grand recipe for muscular masculinity, continues Marson's insistence on unsettling male privilege and revealing the gendered expectations of women's lives. While Kipling's poem inscribes the ethos of imperial masculinity *par excellence*, Marson's parody consciously appropriates this framework in order to communicate the consciously anti-heroic role of a 'wife worth-while'. The apologies to Kipling and to Shakespeare at the end of the parodies do not signal the filial relationship with indifference. Although such explicit intertextuality may suggest that the meanings in operation here can only come into 'play' because of their textual antecedents, the counter-textuality of these poems illustrates that Marson's relationship to tradition is not passive or derivative.

In 'Going to Market,' the positive and sympathetic portrait of the old woman who must work to survive attempts to bring the reality of Jamaican women's life into literature. However, although this poem does not sentimentalize its black female subject, there is a sense in which, as detached observer, the narrator translates her hardships into acts of poetic and moral inspiration. In other poems, Marson finds a poetic language capable of delivering Jamaican women's voices in more immediate form. 'Gettin' De Spirit' records the spiritual and social congregation of women with no formal apparatus to mediate their utterance. Indeed, the command 'Join the chorus' seems to issue a call for sisterly solidarity both within and beyond the page.

'The Stone Breakers' also offers direct access to women's voices as they share the sense of mortal pain and futility which constitutes their lives as a white man's work machine. Their capacity for resilience and endurance is not emotionally indulged, but rather the practical necessities of sustaining their children that the poem overhears not only implicate the exploitation of the poor by the wealthy, and black Jamaicans by white, but also the self-indulgence of their male partners. In 'My Philosophy', the simple ethic of female solidarity spoken by the women presents a stark contrast to the complex hierarchies of difference constructed by colonialism which dictate their lives. In both poems it is the direct deliverance of the spoken word onto the page which is significant as it is an act of giving value and worth to people whose lives and thoughts have been systematically neglected and silenced.

Beyond the black burden

Nothing in 'Another Mould' (1931), a quiet poetic affirmation of black beauty, would prepare readers for the extraordinary poem by Marson that appeared in July 1933 in *The Keys* magazine that she edited in London for the League of Coloured Peoples. 'Nigger' voices a resentment and fury unique within her work. The word 'nigger,' repeated thirteen times in the poem, literally forces itself brutally upon the reader. However, the poem's insistent repetition of the second person, 'you', is equally significant and serves as a substitute term of denigration. It is not the dehumanised black subject who must answer to accusations of inferiority or bestiality here, but the white population, who must claim a contemptible past.

A consciousness of being subjected to the imperial gaze is also present in 'Little Boys', along with the interrogative structure that again directs the injustice and the twisted logic of racism towards the reader. This formal strategy and the preoccupation with voices speaking from a dislocated context, finds its fullest articulation in 'Little Brown Girl'. The poem's title both travesties Blake's 'innocent song', 'The Little Black Boy', and hints at the title of Marson's unpublished *Autobiography of a Brown Girl* which was also written during her time in London. Although the poem stages two voices, that of the little brown girl and a white English man, the persistent second-person questioning of the white English subject creates a sense of hostility and intimidation, disrupting the antiphonal structure anticipated by the interrogative form, with a monologue of conflated ignorance and prejudice. When the voice of the little brown girl does emerge, it speaks an alternative monologue rather than a response. Isolated in the 'white, white city', the (non)encounter refuses the possibility for meaningful cross-cultural communication.

In 'Cinema Eyes', as in 'Kinky Hair Blues', the female subject is compelled to sacrifice any belief in her own physical beauty before the act of integration into the heterosexual racist society can take place. Consciously styled around a movie-style drama, this poem not only offers an exploration of the cinema's promotion of white beauty, but also counters this commoditised ideology, by promoting black beauty. In 'Black Is Fancy', it is the false icon of white beauty which is sacrificed and the poem represents a genesis of self identity in which the young black woman both 'sees' herself and begins to believe in herself – claiming an uncompromised subjectivity. 'Black Burden' also bridges Marson's exposition of racism and her focus on the black person's ability to thrive outside of racist society. It powerfully articulates the problems of claiming and expressing a self which is always already defined, but it also works towards this process. Referring to herself in the third person, the black girl appropriates her objectification in order to resist the burden of definition. The 'I am black' which prefaced the nature of her struggle and explained her behaviour is now erased, as she understands her identity is not defined by race.

One of her most economical verses, 'Politeness' offers an alternative commentary on Blake's poem, this time an ironic inversion of its 'liberalism'. While Blake's poem allows its black subject to plead for equal recognition on the basis that 'I am black, but O! my soul is white', the inverted logic on which Marson's version of the poem is premised invites us to read 'Rudeness' for 'Politeness', challenging the redemptive approach to racism that had also characterised her own earlier writings.

Poems of the Blues

Marson's blues poems represent a significant poetic achievement within their historical moment as they are a rare example of literary work that explores the aesthetic possibilities of Jamaican speech rhythms. Drawing on the African-American genre that developed from the blending of slave spirituals and call and response songs, Marson breaks from the anglocentric meters and forms that shape much of her other poetry. The unpredictable, contingent nature of the blues form, along with its propensity to voice raw human emotions, provides a structure not only for expressing but also for transforming the suffering and negative consciousness of the oppressed subject. In these poems, Marson is able to give voice to both oppression and resistance and, most importantly, to reach towards a culturally specific language which articulates a people's emotions and thoughts in their own terms.

In 'Canefield Blues', the stylized pathos offers a means of expression for the emotional torture of the plantation worker's existence, asserting the affective life of the workers which is denied by the employers, and the capitalist demands of white society. In 'Lonesome Blues' the more mischievous aspect of the blues appears as the 'lone' female subject of this poem ends her song not with despair but with humour. 'Kinky Hair Blues,' one of Marson's most technically accomplished and politically compelling poems, exploits the emotional three-point turns of the blues. The poem confronts the way in which a black woman's sense of 'self' is disfigured by the idealization of white physical beauty. It is significant then that the black female subject of this poem says that she does not feel inherently unhappy with her own appearance but is forced to acquiesce to the patriarchal version of her destiny, succumbing to the need for male approval. All the same, the blues form and language enables a point of reference outside of the colonial and patriarchal value system for the internal resistance of the black female consciousness to be expressed.

Poems for the People

Most 'occasional' Jamaican poetry that was anthologised and given cultural validity during the first half of the twentieth-century chronicled the visits of the British Royal family or other such 'significant' visitors to the island. Constance Hollar's *Songs of Empire* which was published to mark the visit of the Prince of Wales and Prince George in 1931 is a useful example. In this respect, as in others, Marson's work makes a significant departure. Rather than recording events that relate or celebrate dominant or official 'colonial' history in poetic form, her poetry summons incidents, people and alliances that the colonial gaze would choose to avoid.

In some of the poems collected here, the tributes are to cherished friends or organisations, such as the novelist 'Winifred Holtby', whom Marson had met through her association with the British Commonwealth League. In other works, her poetry serves more particularly and pointedly as a form of historical intervention. In both 'At the Prison Gates' and 'For Joe and Ben', Marson offers what Foucault would call a 'counter-memory' of the violence and oppression that has been excluded from colonial histories. Published in 1937, 'At the Prison Gates' provides an instance of such counter-memory in its chronicle of the desperate urban poverty experienced amongst the working classes in Jamaica during the Depression and more particularly the incident when men literally asked to be 'imprisoned' in order to be fed.

This delivery of localised memory to the status of history is made much more explicit in 'To Joe and Ben' which has the explanatory note in parenthesis – 'Brutally murdered in April 1937 at Addis Abbaba by the Italians'. This poem refers specifically to the execution of Joseph and Benjamin Martin, the two sons of Dr Charles Martin, the Abyssinian minister in London, by the Italians in 1937, after their capture in Wollega. In this respect, the poem is an elegy to these lives taken by colonial violence. However, the poem's referencing of this conflict also brings to light an important and often overlooked historical cause for political discontent in the Caribbean region. The betrayal of Abyssinia by England in 1935 and the failure of the League of Nations to protect this fragile state led to the brief but bloody Second Italo–Abyssinian War.

While many of the most striking poems in *The Moth and The Star* focus on the distance that opens up in human encounters because of unjust and inadequate understandings of race, 'The Stranger' also represents the possibility of a more benign and intimate relationship that is able to acknowledge difference without inscribing inequality. Ideas of inclusivity function differently in some of these poems, such as 'The Peanut Boy' from *Heights and Depths*, that offer a textual presence to the lives of the working-class and the poor rural folk whose ways of life and voices also came to political notice in the 1930s with the formation of labour parties and trade unions and a nationalism that sought to represent these people in both senses. Again though, there is a distinctive marbling of poetic registers that refuses a progressive narrative of poetic development. The assured and irreverent perspective of 'Quashie Comes to London', that shifts the focus from a colonial version of black people's experience found in 'Little Brown Girl' to Quashie's Jamaican perspective of English society sits in the same volume as the rather flat, lifeless stylisation of 'The Banjo Boy'.

Probably the most significant addition that *Towards the Stars* makes to Marson's poetic work is a small body of poems that represent the experience of living through war-torn London. In 'Interlude' the composed verbal structure of accruing clauses creates the sense of a terror fully anticipated but as yet unknowable. This same sense of composure within the shadow of menace gives shape to 'In the Darkness', although here it is the spiritual comfort that she expresses in so many of her earlier works that still sustains. Both 'Dawn' and 'Frozen' represent the loss and degradation of human life that the conflict has brought. The unpublished work, 'The Seed', written in the 1950s when Marson was resident in Washington D.C., makes a direct reference to the acute sensitization to violence that the experience of living through the war had engendered. Yet however accurate in their emotional register these works of war appear, for Marson, the ideal of peace and of simple but unconditional human recognition remained an urgent and unquestionable goal throughout her life, both in Jamaica and England. In 'There Will Come A Time' and 'He Called Us Brethren', Marson summons the uncomplicated and yet somehow unattainable vision of a world free from false divisions. These works powerfully articulate her sense of commitment to this possibility and, importantly, they register an optimism that always informed her political consciousness and enabled her life as a poet to enrich the causes she was so passionately involved in.

REFERENCES

Brown, Lloyd, *West Indian Poetry* (London: Heinemann Educational Books Ltd, 1984).

DeCaires Narain, *Contemporary Caribbean Women's Poetry: Making Style* (London: Routledge, 2002).

Donnell, Alison 'Sentimental Subversions: the poetics and politics of devotion in the poetry of Una Marson' in *Kicking Daffodils: essays on*

Twentieth-Century Women's Poetry, Vicki Bertram (ed) (Edinburgh: Edinburgh University Press (1997): pp. 113-124.

—— 'Contradictory (W)omens? Gender Consciousness in the Poetry of Una Marson', *Kunapipi*, XVII (1995): pp. 43-58.

——— 'Una Marson: anti-colonialism, feminism and a forgotten struggle' in West Indian Intellectuals in Britain, Bill Schwarz (ed.) (Manchester University Press, 2003), pp. 114-131.

Fanon, Frantz, *Black Skin White Masks* (London: MacGibbon & Kee, London, 1968): p. 150.

Ford-Smith, Honor, (1983-1985) 'Una Marson: Black Nationalist And Feminist Writer', Research Project: Women and Development, Institute of Social Studies, The Hague.

Hughes, Langston and Arna Bontemps (eds.) *The Poetry of the Negro 1746-1949* (New York: Doubleday & Company, Inc. 1949).

Jarrett-Macauley, Delia, *The Life of Una Marson, 1905-65* (Manchester: Manchester University Press, 1998).

Marson, Una, *Tropic Reveries* (Kingston, 1930).

—— *Heights and Depths* (Kingston, 1931).

—— 'Nigger', *The Keys*, July 1933, pp. 8-9.

—— *The Moth and the Star* (Kingston, 1937).

—— *Towards the Stars* (Kent, 1945).

McFarlane, J. E. Clare, 'The Challenge of Our Time' (address delivered at the opening of the twenty-fourth Session of the Poetry League of Jamaica, Institute of Jamaica, 31 January 1935) in *The Challenge of Our Time* (Kingston, Jamaica, 1945).

—— *A Literature In The Making* (Kingston, Pioneer Press, 1956).

Reid, Victor S., 'The Cultural Revolution in Jamaica After 1938' (address delivered at the Institute of Jamaica, [1978])

Smilowitz, Erika, 'Una Marson: Woman Before Her Time', *Jamaica Journal*, 16, (1983).

—— ' "Weary of Life and All My Heart's Dull Pain": The Poetry of Una Marson' in *Critical Issues In West Indian Literature* edited by Erika Smilowitz and Roberta Knowles (Iowa, 1984): pp. 19-32.

Snaith, Anna, '"Little Brown Girl" in a "White, White City": Una Marson and London,' *Tulsa Women's Studies* (27.1, 2008): pp. 95-114.

Swanzy, Henry, 'The Literary Situation in the Caribbean,', *Books Abroad*, vol. 30, no. 3, (Summer 1956): pp. 266-74: 271.

TROPIC REVERIES

LONGING

The roses long for sunshine
And rain and cooling dew,
The songbirds long for summer,
And love, I long for you.

I long to have you near me,
To see your smile divine,
To hear you softly whisper
'Beloved you are mine.'

I long for your caresses,
For just one tender kiss,
To thrill my soul with rapture
And fill my heart with bliss.

Beloved I am longing,
When shall this yearning cease,
And I be resting by you
In perfect calm and peace?

(*Tropic Reveries*, p. 17)

RENUNCIATION

For me the sunbeams dance and dart
And songbirds sing with merry heart,
For me the winds are whispering low
And laughing flowers in hedges grow.

For me the brook runs merrily
With soothing song to seek the sea,
For me Diana sheds her light
And steadfast stars shine thro' the night.

For me the waves of ocean sigh
Or dance with sunbeams darting by,
For me the shades of twilight fall
And beauty doth the earth enthral:

But not for me what most I crave, —
To call thee mine, — to be thy slave.

(*Tropic Reveries*, p. 20. Anthologised in the *Routledge Reader in Caribbean Literature* (1996), p. 128, co-edited by Alison Donnell and Sarah Lawson-Welsh)

IN VAIN

In vain I build me stately mansions fair,
And set thee as my king upon the throne,
And place a lowly stool beside thee there,
Thus, as thy slave to come into my own.

In vain I deck the halls with roses sweet
And strew the paths with petals rich and rare,
And list with throbbing heart sounds of thy feet,
The welcome voice that tells me thou art near.

In vain I watch the dawn break in the sky
And hope that thou wilt come with coming day:
Alas, Diana calmly sails on high,
But thou, king of my heart, art far away.

In vain one boon from life's great store I crave,
No more the king comes to his waiting slave.

(*Tropic Reveries*: p. 27. Anthologised in the *Routledge Reader in Caribbean Literature* (1996), p. 128)

INCOMPLETE

What matters it tonight that all is bright,
That laughter and glad music fill the air,
That crowds on pleasure bent feel great delight
And Christmas bells are ringing everywhere.

What matters it though friends are gathering round
To wish the best that Christmas day can bring,
That peace and love within their hearts abound,
And that they bid me still to dance and sing.

What matters it though gifts be strewn on me,
Though loving greetings come with every mail,
And naught but things to please and cheer I see, –
All these to bring me gladness sadly fail:

For though the great wide world lay at my feet,
Without your smile my life is incomplete.

(*Tropic Reveries*, p. 28)

46

I AM CONTENT

I am content to love you to the end,
To have you fill my thoughts both night and day,
Though not on me your fondest love you spend
And in your thoughts I hold but little sway.

I am content to listen for your call,
To hasten or delay at your behest,
Tho' when I need you most as shadows fall,
It seems you still must linger with the rest.

I am content if only you are glad,
If to your heart there comes no cruel pain.
Though life is drear and when my heart is sad
In silent prayer I long for you in vain:

Oh love, I am content, although I know
The years will bring but emptiness and woe.

(*Tropic Reveries*, p. 29)

VOWS

Make me no vows, beloved, do not say
That come what may your love will never change,
Oh do not vow that you will love for aye,
That naught can evermore your heart estrange.

Make me no vows against the coming years
For who can tell what changes they may bring?
They may be filled with laughter or with tears,
To some new soul your tender heart may cling.

Make me no vows, so that you love me now
With all the ardour of your loving soul –
What need have we of promise or of vow,
What is to be is written in His scroll:

Oh love me while you may, for who can tell
How soon the time may come to say farewell.

(*Tropic Reveries*, p. 30)

I CANNOT TELL

I cannot tell why I who once was gay
And never knew the burden of a sigh
Now sit and pass the weary hours away,
And never have a care for what goes by.

I cannot tell why oft the teardrops rise
And my sad heart lies leaden in my breast,
And in my mind these anxious thoughts arise
For no more am I happy with the rest.

I cannot tell why life is not the same
And my heart answers not to music's plea,
Or why I start whene'er I hear your name
And in my dreams no other face I see:

I cannot tell why I should wish to die,
Now that the time has come to say goodbye.

(*Tropic Reveries*, p. 31)

LOVE'S LAMENT

I cannot let you hold me in your arms
And listen while you talk of trivial things;
It pains my heart thus to resist your charms
And see the longings of my soul take wings.

I cannot feel the pressure of your hands
Without the wish to hold them to my lips,
I have no strength to face life's big demands
While daily from my heart your image slips,

I cannot bear the thought of losing you.
Yet still your presence brings me bitter pain.
The happy days gone by we will not rue –
Their tender mem'ries still to us remain;

But oh my heart, I cannot bid you stay,
Though as you go you take my life away.

(*Tropic Reveries*, p. 32)

LOVE'S FAREWELL

'Tis best that we should say farewell for aye,
And never meet again in fond embrace;
Away I go, some thousand miles away,
And I may nevermore behold your face.

'Tis best that we should part; let us forgo
The farewell hour, oh love, I cannot hear
Those words fall from your lips altho' I know
I nevermore may see your face so dear.

Oh please forgive this coward heart of mine,
That cannot meet the pain in your dear eyes,
And rest my trembling hands once more in thine
And stem the tears that in my heart arise.

Oh love, I know you would not have me go,
But be content, the Fates have willed it so.

(*Tropic Reveries*, p. 33)

51

I KNOW NOT

I know not where thou lingerest tonight,
Or where thy footsteps strayed the livelong day,
Or whither though wilt go tomorrow night, –
I only know that thou art far away.

I know not now who sees thee when thou smilest,
And hears the mellow music of thy voice,
Nor how the fleeting hours thou beguilest;
It may be that once more thou hast no choice.

I know not if one little thought of me
Sometimes comes softly stealing to your heart,
Nor if a vestige of regret there be
Now that, beloved one, we are apart:

But this I know, my love shall follow thee
Throughout all time into eternity.

(*Tropic Reveries*, p. 34)

ABSENCE

What shall I do to bribe the hours of day
And long, long hours of night to hasten on,
To quickly come and faster pass away,
Nor lengthen out the hours while you are gone?

How shall I bid the moon to stay her beams
And linger on awhile until you come,
Or banish from my mind these fitful dreams,
That in my weary heart have made their home?

O present day and due returning night,
Speed, speed away, right quickly don your wings,
I thee implore; come make a hasty flight,
My longing heart beats many questionings;

And never, night or day, will be at rest
Until once more I hold thee to my breast.

(Tropic Reveries, p. 35)

ANSWER

Love of my soul, I love you
With love I can't express,
But you must know beloved
It means unhappiness.

'Tis true, how true, I need you
More than all else beside,
What would I give my darling
To linger by your side.

I'm jealous of the breezes
That play about your hair,
I'm jealous of the sunbeams
To which you are so near.

Beloved, how I love you
Nor tongue nor pen can tell,
Oh heart of mine, be silent.
I love you but too well.

And yet I cannot grant you
The boon you ask of me, –
Oh cruel fate that hinders
Nor makes this captive free.

And can I thus deny you
When but your slave am I?
And yet I must beloved,
Though with a broken sigh.

I know you do not love me
And it is better so,
Because my bitter anguish
Your tender heart might know.

And when I give beloved
I give with both my hands,
Nor ever should recapture
The prize your love demands.

Dear, since you do not love me
And our ways lie apart,
Forget how much I love you
And I will do my part.

And now you know my secret
Oh, ask of me no more
Lest I forget and open
My heart's firm closed door.

Ask me no more, beloved,
For I can ne'er be thine,
Nor have the fates decreed it
That some day you'll be mine.

Ask me no more my darling;
What pain thus to deny
The idol of my vision
For whom I daily sigh!

I must refuse, beloved,
Or soil my soul with sin,
In yielding to your passion, –
Your love I may not win.

Our lives must drift apart, dear,
Forget me, it is best;
But, oh, the pain and heartache
That never will know rest.

(*Tropic Reveries*, p.51-3)

JAMAICA

Thou Fairest Island of the Western Sea,
What tribute has the Muse to pay to thee?
Oh, that some tender lay she could inspire
That we might sing thy praises and ne'er tire.
Oh lovely Island where the sun shines bright
And scarce one week withholds her cheery light;
No chilly winter wind doth o'er thee blow,
No fields and streams are covered o'er with snow,
But one grand summer all the long year through
Dost thou enjoy beneath a sky of blue.

Among thy woods the birds with carols gay
From morn till night are merrily at play;
The hum of bees upon the flowering trees
Makes sweetest music with the summer breeze.
The fields are covered o'er with Daisies bright
Which nod their pretty heads in sheer delight;
By babbling brooks the shady palms arise,
While wandering near, earth seems a Paradise.

The brilliance of the myriad stars by night
Unto the weary traveller giveth light;
Among thy woods the flitting fireflies
Form one grand starland with their fiery eyes.
And when Diana rising o'er yon hill
Sheds her pale light, while all the earth is still,
Ah, then, what bliss to wander hand in hand
Like lovers 'neath the bowers in Fairyland.

All hail to thee! Fair Island of the West,
Where thy dear people are forever blest
With beauteous gifts from nature's blessed hand,
Lavished in rich profusion o'er the land.
Welcome be all who journey many a mile

To share the joys of this our lovely Isle:
Fond nature still invites, – 'Come, be my guest
And I will give thee gladness, peace and rest!'

(*Tropic Reveries*, pp. 60-61. Anthologised in the *Routledge Reader in Caribbean Literature* (1996), p.130.)

THE SINGING PILGRIM

I was sitting by the wayside
Restive in the waiting car,
For I longed to hasten homewards,
I had journeyed from afar.

Dark the sky o'erhead and cloudy,
And the night wind whispered low,
Naught relieved the inky blackness
But the silent flitting glow

Of the ever restless fireflies,
Dancing madly here and there,
As I sat amid the silence
That to me seemed everywhere.

What was that? The sound of singing
Coming nearer and more near,
Sadly sweet, so full of pathos
Was the song that reached me there.

Not a sound was heard of footsteps:
Just the sweet and plaintive strain
Sung by someone in the darkness,
Sung in accents clear and plain

"Must I go – and empty handed?
Must I meet my Saviour so?
Not one soul with which to greet Him?
Must I empty handed go?"

Suddenly a short slim figure
Stepped into the path of light
Streaming from the silent motor,
And I wondered at the sight.

'Twas the figure of a woman
Going down the hill of life –
Her brown face was worn and wrinkled
By life's strenuous toil and strife.

On her head she bore a basket
Balanced there composedly,
Silently her bare feet moving
While her empty hands swung free.

Eagerly I gazed upon her,
That lone traveller of the night,
And it seemed but one brief second
Ere she vanished from my sight.

Vanished once more in the darkness,
Vanished, singing soft and low;
"Must I go and empty handed
Must I meet my Saviour so?"

Every word seemed to be uttered
From a heart with love aglow, –
"Not one soul with which to greet Him,
Must I empty handed go?"

Softly and more soft it sounded,
As the singer journeyed on;
Soon was gone from sight and hearing
That lone singer and her song.

On she passed; her sweet song faded
Like the twilight into night;
But as long as life is with me
I shall ne'er forget that sight.

How unconscious was the singer
That her tuneful song that day
In another soul had wakened
Thoughts that would forever stay.

Thoughts of Christ, the wondrous Saviour
Whom one day we hope to meet;
Would I take no comrade with me?
Cast no trophies at His feet?

And I prayed for grace and wisdom
To proclaim my Saviour's love,
And to help some weary wanderer
Reach that better land above.

And I prayed too that the singer
Should not meet her Lord alone,
But that those she loved would gather
With her round the great White throne.

Then I went along the highway
Hearing still the sweet refrain,
And throughout my life's long journey
It shall in my heart remain.

Oh, I must be very thoughtful,
For the things I say and do
After this my life is ended,
Surely meet with me anew.

Just a word, a thought, an action
May cause untold good or ill,
I must live to help, not hinder,
As I journey up life's hill.

(*Tropic Reveries*, p. 62-5)

TO HAMPTON

Sweet Hampton – fairest school of all the Isle,
Where happily I sojourned for a while –
And passed those happy years so free from pain,
What would I give to dwell with thee again?

Oh glorious School among the hills so high,
Where sunsets glow upon the tropic sky,
Where birds among the woods with carols gay
Hail the first splendours of the coming day.

Thou dearest school of all my youthful days,
Oh that the muse would grant me voice to praise
Thy charms, thy rare delights, thy bowers of ease
Which often made e'en Latin verbs to please.

For when at last the day's full tasks were done,
Each afternoon, long ere the set of sun,
We gladly clamoured out and gathered round
To tennis, hockey, games or chat profound,

Or hand in hand to wander in the shade
And search for orchids through each hill and glade,
To sit beneath the trees in friendship sweet
And hear the nightingales each other greet,

Or yet to wander lonely 'mong the trees
And hear the music of the birds and bees –
And drink from nature all the rest and peace
That in the haunts of nature never cease.

Then the great bell that told when games were done
Summoned us all within the walls to come –
One hour of silent study, this would close
Our busy day, and bring us sweet repose.

And on the last night of each happy week,
No class room – but the splendid hall we'd seek,
All "dolled up" in our pretty clothes we'd go
With joy to trip the light fantastic toe.

And on the Sabbath day all dressed in white,
We'd sing the hymns of praise with all our might,
And when the evening shadows gathered round,
We'd list to songs and harmonies of sound.

Such were thy charms: and oft when cares oppress,
And sorrows and dull cares my heart distress,
Fond memory turns to those glad scenes again –
Those gladsome days that could not long remain.

Ah me, the cares of Latin and of French,
And of long hours spent upon the bench,
The toils of writing prose and conning rhymes
To us, no doubt, did seem large ones at times.

But in the hard world, when we take our place,
And strife and toil we each one have to face,
Ah then, we smile at what seemed such large cares,
And those small things that often caused us tears.

How oft in dreams I live those days again,
Chasing a hockey ball with might and main,
Or sit and list without a thought of fear
To dearest Mona reading great Shakespeare.

Sweet Hampton, still with grateful loyal heart
We think of thee; and in life's busy mart,
We bless thy founders and thy Head whose care
Hath made thee what thou art, a school most dear.

(*Tropic Reveries*, p. 69-70)

TO WED OR NOT TO WED

To wed, or not to wed: that is the question:
Whether 'tis nobler in the mind to suffer
The fret and loneliness of spinsterhood
Or to take arms against the single state
And by marrying end it? To wed; to match,
No more; yet by this match to say we end
The heartache and the thousand natural shocks
That flesh is heir to; 'tis a consummation
Devoutly to be wish'd. To wed, to match;
To match, perchance mismatch: aye, there's the rub;
For in that match what dread mishaps may come,
When we have shuffled off this single state
For wedded bliss: there's the respect
That makes singleness of so long life,
For who'd forego the joys of wife and mother,
The pleasures of devotion, of sacrifice and love,
The blessings of a home and all home means,
The restful sympathy of soul to soul,
The loved ones circling round at eventide
When she herself might gain all these
With a marriage vow? Who would fardels bear
To pine and sigh under a single life
But that the dread of something after marriage,
That undiscovered nature, from whose ways
One scarce can sever, puzzles the will,
And makes us rather cling to single bliss
Than barter that we know for things unsure?
Thus dreadful doubt makes cowards of us all
And thus the native hue of resolution
Is sicklied o'er with the pale case of thought,
And matrimonial rites, and wedded life
With this regard their currents turn away
And lose the name of action.

(With apologies to Shakespeare.)

(*Tropic Reveries*, p. 81-2)

IF

If you can keep him true when all about you
The girls are making eyes and being kind,
If you can make him spend the evenings with you
When fifty Jims and Jacks are on his mind;
If you can wait and not be tired by waiting,
Or when he comes at one, be calm and sleep,
And do not oversleep, but early waking
Smile o'er the tea cups, and ne'er think to weep.

If you can love and not make love your master,
If you can serve yet do not be his slave.
If you can hear bright tales and quit them faster,
And, for your peace of mind, think him no knave;
If you can bear to hear the truth you tell him
Twisted around to make you seem a fool,
Or see the Capstan on your bureau burning
And move the noxious weed, and still keep cool.

If you can make one heap of all he gives you
And try to budget so that it's enough,
And add, subtract and multiply the issue,
So that the Grocer will not cut up rough;
If you can force your dress, and hat, and stocking
To serve their turn long after they are worn,
And pass the "sales", and do not think it shocking
To wear a garment that has once been torn:

If you can walk when he takes out the Ford
And teaches girls to drive before you learn,
And list to tales of tyres without a wry word,
And let him feel you're glad for his return:

If you can fill the unforgiving minute
With sixty seconds work and prayer and smile,
Yours is the world and everything that's in it,
And what is more, you'll be a wife worth while.

(*With apologies to Kipling.*)

(*The Cosmopolitan* , October, 1929, p.193; Tropic *Reveries*, p. 83-4)

THE POET'S HEART

Think not that those who spend their time
In building up the lofty rhyme
Are often of another clime
Than those who pass them by.

They differ not, but in degree: —
More deeply feel all that they see.
They hold to nature the great key,
And ope' the portals wide.

What some will pass and scarce admire
Just sets the poet's soul afire;
In praise of it he ne'er can tire,
In rapture he is lost.

He knows that many hearts are sad
That need someone to make them glad;
They would be happy if they had
A sympathising friend.

His poet's heart goes out to these,
Their sorrows and their woes he sees
By words of comfort oft he frees
The weary burdened heart.

Oh soul that mid earth's darkest hours
Still sings of hope among earth's bowers,
Sing on: thy songs bring richest showers
Of blessings unto me.

(*Tropic Reveries*, p. 87)

HEIGHTS AND DEPTHS

THE SPEEDWELL

I love the little speedwell flowers
That grow beside my door,
They close their eyes and go to sleep
Just as the clock strikes four.

But at the songbird's waking cry,
They open their blue eyes,
Eyes bluer than the ocean's breast,
And fairer than the skies.

One day the busy honeybee
Came just at break of day,
The speedwells had scarce ope'd their eyes
Ere he was on the way.

"Awake, awake, my loves," he said
And gently kissed each,
"I love your eyes of dainty blue,
You rob my heart of speech."

Then, with a promise to return,
He on his errands went,
The speedwells laughed and whispered low,
"This has been some event."

"He has not been to us for weeks
He has so many loves,
But how can we resist his charms
Though often far he roves?"

And then they laughed and danced about
The while I loved them more,
I hope that I shall always see
Fair speedwells at my door.

(*Heights and Depths*, p. 6)

69

NATURE'S HEART

Give me a life of indolence and ease
Close to the heart of Nature. When I please,
Let me revisit man's relentless mart
And feel the pulse of her swift throbbing heart.

Let me be free to wander by yon stream,
And sit beneath the trees and dream and dream
With song of birds to soothe my heart's dull pain,
And join the rushing river's sweet refrain.

And let me listen while the dainty flowers
Whisper and laugh away the golden hours,
And learn from them how they such fragrance give
Although so brief a time on earth they live.

Let me adore the beauty of a tree
So graceful and so full of majesty,
And learn the secret that to birds belongs
How I may lift life's burden with a song.

Oh give me heaven's blue above my head,
And fragrant wild flowers on a mossy bed;
And when I seek again life's busy mart,
May Nature's peace sustain my fevered heart.

(*Heights and Depths*, p. 9)

THE MEETING OF THE CLOUDS

One day upon the soft green grass
  I lay in idle mood
The sunshine glittered on the leaves,
  All things to me seemed good.

The sky bore but two fleecy clouds
  One east, the other west,
And each seemed lonely wondering there,
  And full of vague unrest.

And as I watched, these fleecy clouds
  Towards each other drew,
And in what seemed a moment's space,
  How close to each they grew.

Then, in one eager breathless rush,
  They melted into one;
And lingered but a moment there,
  And were forever gone.

The sky became a cloudless blue,
  I turned towards the sea,
And bore with me a tender thought
  Of you, dear heart, and me.

E'en so our souls would fain unite
  In one long, fond embrace,
And slip from off this weary earth
  To some ethereal place.

But now our bodies intervene,
  Yet there will come a time
When, as the clouds became but one,
  Your soul will join with mine;

71

In some fond place where spirits meet,
    We shall know endless joy,
No weariness of earth and flesh
    Shall then our peace annoy.

(*Heights and Depths*, p. 15)

JAMAICA

J ust a lovely little jewel floating on fair Carib's breast,
A ll a-glittering in her verdue 'neath a blazing tropic sky.
M ust have been part of Eden, it's so full of peace and rest,
A nd the flowers in their splendour make you feel it's good to die
I n a spot that's so near heaven where one never feels depressed,
'C ause Dame Nature makes you lazy and Dame Fortune lingers nigh,
A nd you feel just like a fledgling in your mother's cosy nest.

(*Heights and Depths*, p. 19)

I CARE NOT

I care not for the sunshine
      or for the silver rain,
I care not for the flowers
      that still to me remain,
I care not for the moonlight
      or for the evening Star,
I care not for the zephyr
      that cometh from afar.
I care not for life's wonders
      unless thou smile on me,
For in thy smile the beauty
      of all the world I see.

(*Heights and Depths*, p. 32)

RESIGNATION

Last night when you said you had to play bridge,
And asked if I like the game,
For a moment it pained me and somehow I thought
That my darling was not just the same.

Play bridge! when each fibre of my aching heart
Yearned just for the touch of your hand,
When naught that the world could give to me then
Could grant me my soul's demand?

What madness came o'er me that made me forget
That only in dreams you are mine –
Altho' from the moment when first we two met,
My heart has been sealed as thine.

Forgive me, beloved; whatever you do
My full heart must praise and condone,
Since out of the great world I have chosen you
And set you as king on my throne.

(*Heights and Depths*, p. 43)

THE PEANUT BOY

Lord, look upon this peanut boy,
He's rough and coarse and rude;
He has been selling all the day,
His words are very crude.

But, Lord, he's worn and weary now,
See how he stands asleep;
His head is resting on the post,
The basket at his feet.

Dear Lord, he has not sold them all,
But he has done his best:
And, while he stands and sleeps awhile,
With sweet dreams make him blest.

And, Lord, when I shall fall asleep
With my tasks incomplete,
Remember I was weary Lord,
And give me peaceful sleep.

(*Heights and Depths*, p. 74)

ANOTHER MOULD

You can talk about your babies
With blue eyes and hair of gold,
But I'll tell you 'bout an angel
That's cast in another mould.

She is brown just like a biscuit
And she has the blackest eyes
That don't for once remind you
Of the blue of tropic skies.

And her hair is black and shiny
And her little teeth are pearls,
She's just a year I'll tell you,
But the best of baby girls.

O, she's sweeter than the sweetest
Of all babies 'neath the sun,
And I feel that I could eat her,
Thinking she's a sugar bun.

O, little ivory babies
Are as sweet as they can be,
But give me my brown skin cherub
Still a-dangling on my knee.

(*Heights and Depths*, p. 77)

IN JAMAICA

O! the sun shines warm in Jamaica,
From one year's end to the next,
The flowers bloom on in Jamaica,
And songbirds are never perplexed;
It's a lazy life that we live here
Tho' we carry a fair share of work;
And tho' the warmth makes us weary,
It's seldom we really do shirk.

O! the darkies smile on in Jamaica,
And whistle or sing all the day;
There's always a song ringing somewhere,
To them it is always bright May.
It's little we need for our comfort,
When we live in a wee cosy cot
In the heart of the hills where kind Nature
Gives all, and the towns are forgot.

O! It's a glorious life in Jamaica
For the man who has merely enough,
But it's a dreary life for the beggars,
And the large slums are all pretty rough.
It's a gay life too for the children
Not poor, and whose skin is light,
But the darker set are striving
And facing a very stiff fight.

O, it's a wonderful life in Jamaica
For the tourists who visit this shore,
There's golf, there's dancing, and swimming,
And charms that they ne'er saw before.

They call it a garden of Eden,
They love the fair hills of St Ann,
And they say on the white sands of Mo. Bay
They get such a wonderful tan!

O, there's beauty in most every country,
And scenes that bring thrills of delight,
But there's no place like sunny Jamaica,
And no people whose hearts are so light.
Should I leave these fair shores for another,
Be that land yet the fairest of all,
I should pine for the hills of Jamaica,
And hasten to answer her call.

(*Heights & Depths*, p. 82. Anthologised in the *Routledge Reader in Caribbean Literature* (1996), pp.131-2)

THERE WILL COME A TIME

Each race that breathes the air of God's fair world
Is so bound up within its little self,
So jealous for material wealth and power
That it forgets to look outside itself
Save when there is some prospect of rich gain;
Forgetful yet that each and every race
Is brother unto his, and in the heart
Of every human being excepting none,
There lies the selfsame love, the selfsame fear,
The selfsame craving for the best that is,
False pride and petty prejudice prevail
Where love and brotherhood should have full sway.

When shall this cease? 'Tis God alone who knows;
But we who see through this hypocrisy
And feel the blood of black and white alike
Course through our veins as our strong heritage
Must range ourselves to build the younger race.
What matter that we be as cagéd birds
Who beat their breasts against the iron bars
Till blood-drops fall, and in heartbreaking songs
Our souls pass out to God? These very words,
In anguish sung, will mightily prevail.
We will not be among the happy heirs
Of this grand heritage – but unto us
Will come their gratitude and praise,
And children yet unborn will reap in joy
What we have sown in tears.

                    For there will come
A time when all the races of the earth
Grown weary of the inner urge for gain,
Grown sick of all the fatness of themselves
And all their boasted prejudice and pride

Will see this vision that now comes to me.
Aye, there will come a time when every man
Will feel that other men are brethren unto him –
When men will look into each other's hearts
And souls, and not upon their skin and brain,
And difference in the customs of the race.
Though I should live a hundred years or more
I should not see this time, but while I live,
'Tis mine to share in this gigantic task
Of oneness for the world's humanity.

(*Heights and Depths*, p. 95)

THE KEYS

NIGGER

They called me "Nigger"
Those little white urchins.
They laughed and shouted
As I passed along the street,
They flung it at me:
"Nigger! Nigger! Nigger!"

What made me keep my fingers
From choking the words in their throats?
What made my face grow hot,
The blood boil in my veins
And tears spring to my eyes?
What made me go to my room
And sob my heart away
Because white urchins
Called me "Nigger"?

What makes the dark West Indian
Fight at being called a Nigger?
What is there in a word
That should strike like a dagger
To the heart of Coloured men
And make them wince?

You of the white skinned Race,
You who profess such innocence,
I'll tell you why 'tis a sin to tell
Your offspring Coloured folks are queer,
Black men are bogies and inferior far
To any creature with a skin made white.

You who feel that you are "sprung
Of earth's first blood", your eyes
Are blinded now with arrogance.
With ruthlessness you seared
My people's flesh, and now you still
Would crush their very soul,
Add fierce insult to vilest injury.

We will not be called "Niggers"
Since this was the favourite curse
Of those who drove the Negroes
To their death in days of slavery.
"A good for nothing Nigger",
"Only one more Nigger gone"
They would repeat as though
He were a chicken or a rat.
That word then meant contempt,
All that was low and base,
And too refined for lower animals.

In later years when singing Negroes
Caused white men to laugh,
And show some interest in their art
They talked of "Nigger Minstrels"
And patronised the Negro,
And laughing at his songs
They could nowise see
The thorns that pierced his heart.
"Nigger" was raised then to a Burlesque Show
And thus from Curse to Clown progressed
A coloured man was cause for merriment.
And though to-day he soars in every field
Some shrunken souls still say
"Look at that Nigger there
As though they saw a green bloodhound
Or a pink puppy.

God keep my soul from hating such mean souls,
God keep my soul from hating
Those who preach the Christ
And say with churlish smile
"This place is not for 'Niggers'."
God save their souls from this great sin
Of hurting human hearts that live
And think and feel in unison
With all humanity.

(July 1933, pp. 8-9). Anthologised in the *Routledge Reader in Caribbean Literature* (1996), pp. 140-2)

EDUCATION

In South Africa £25 per head per annum is spent on educating the white child. The government gives a subsidy of £2 3s. 7d. per head to the missionary bodies who have undertaken the education of 300,000 black children of the 1,100,000 who should be educated. (W.G. Ballinger at W.I.L. CONFERENCE)

It must be by oppression; and, for my part,
I know no personal cause to spurn at them,
But for my countrymen. They would be learned: –
How that might change their nature, there's the question,
It is the bright day that brings forth the adder;
And that craves wary walking. Teach him? – that; –
And then, I grant, we put a sting in him,
That at his will he may do danger with.
The abuse of learning is when it is given
To subject races: And, to speak truth of Negroes,
I have known when they have turned to serve us
Once they are taught. But 'tis a common proof
That lowliness is young ambitious ladder
Whereto the climber upward turns his face:
But when he once attains the utmost round,
He then unto the ladder turns his back,
Looks in the clouds, scorning the base degrees
By which he did ascend: So Negroes may:
Then, lest they may, prevent. And, since the quarrel
Will bear no colour for the thing they are,
Fashion it thus; that what they are, when learned
Would run to these and these extremities:
And therefore, think them as the serpents
Which, hatch'd, would as their kind grow mischievous;
And keep them ignorant.

With Apologies to Shakespeare

(*The Keys*, Jan-March 1935, p. 53)

THE MOTH AND THE STAR

VAGABOND CREED

I said by the stars you are wrong,
By the streams and the woods and the flowers,
By the birds that give freely their song,
By the trees that are bathed by the showers.

It is futile to rush and to dash,
To toil every hour for gold,
It is idle to make a great "splash"
And earth's fleeting joys try to hold.

It is better to muse all alone
For hours in Nature's domain,
Than to sit on a bright gilded throne
Or dwell in unrest just for gain.

It is better to feel hunger's call
While the soul can mount up with wings,
Than to feast in a glorious hall
And gossip of mean petty things.

For the body is merely a cloak,
It's the spirit and soul that live on,
And I am a real happy bloke
For the whole world to me doth belong.

(*The Moth and The Star*, p. 8)

LITTLE BROWN GIRL

Little brown girl
Why do you wander alone
About the streets
Of the great city
Of London?

Why do you start and wince
When white folk stare at you?
Don't you think they wonder
Why a little brown girl
Should roam about their city
Their white, white city?

Little brown girl
Why did you leave
Your little sunlit land
Where we sometimes go
To rest and get brown
So we may look healthy?

What are you seeking,
What would you have?
In London town
There are no laughing faces,
People frown if one really laughs,
Everyone is quiet,
That is respectable;
There's nothing picturesque
To be seen in the streets,
Nothing but people clad
In Coats, Coats, Coats,
Coats in autumn, winter and spring,
And often in the Summer –
A city of coated people
But little to charm the eye.

And the folks are all white –
White, white, white,
And they all seem the same
As they say that Negroes seem.
No pretty copper coloured skins,
No black and bronze and brown
No chocolate and high brown girls
Clad in smart colours
To blend with the complexion,
And wearing delicate
Dainty shoes on dainty feet
That one can admire.
No friendly country folk
Parading the city
With bare feet,
Bright attractive bandanas,
Black faces, pearly teeth
And flashing eyes.
No heavy laden donkeys
And weary laden women
Balancing huge baskets
So cleverly on their heads
While they greet each other
And tell of little things
That mean so much to them.

Little brown girl
Do you like the shops
And all the lovely things
In the show windows?
Wouldn't you like a coat
With a fifty pound tag on it
Or one of those little hats
In Bond Street?

Little brown girl
Why do you look so hard
At the Bobbies
And the book stalls
And the City Lights?
Why do you stop and look
At all the pictures
Outside the theatres?
Do you like shows?
Have you theatres
In your country
And from whence are you
Little brown girl?
I guess Africa or India,
Ah no, from some island
in the West Indies,
But isn't that India
All the same?

I heard you speak
To the Bobbie,
You speak good English
Little brown girl,
How is it you speak
English as though it belonged
To you?

Would you like to be white
Little brown girl?
I don't think you would
For you toss your head
As though you are proud
To be brown.

Little brown girl
Don't you feel very strange

To be so often alone
In a crowd of whites?
Do you remember you are brown
Or do you forget?
Or do people staring at you
Remind you of your colour?

Little brown girl
You are exotic
And you make me wonder
All sorts of things
When you stroll about London
Seeking, seeking, seeking.
What are you seeking
To discover in this dismal
City of ours?
From the look in your eyes
Little brown girl
I know it is something
That does not really exist.

(*The Moth and the Star*, pp. 11-3, *Towards the Stars*, pp. 52-6)

HE CALLED US BRETHREN!

I read it in the paper
Yesterday – strange reading.
It was the story of a service
Held annually for Coloured people
In London by their League.
It ran somewhat like this:
The preacher called them brethren
And who were they but coloured folk!
And who was the preacher but English!
He called us brethren and the Press
Was pleased to publish this strange news.

God, if thou didst make
Of one blood all mankind
To dwell upon the face of the earth,
Christ, if Thou didst bleed upon the Cross
To bring the world to God
Let not Thy glorious travail be in vain,
For vain it is when Thy Servant
Commended is for owning us as brethren.

O England, England, heart of an Empire
That reaches to remotest parts of earth,
Beneath thy flag are men in every clime;
How slow thou art to comprehend the truth,
The universal truth that all must learn –
And thou the foremost for thou hast set
Great claim upon the holy words of God.
For greater than all battles
That are fought in freedom's name,
Mightier than ships and planes,
More valiant than the daring deeds
Of heroes, stronger than the bonds
That bind the peoples of one Race

Is that same blood that flows –
That flows alike through black and white
Making us one in Christ.

(*The Moth and the Star*, p. 15)

THE STRANGER

You liked talking to people like me
You said, with a wistful smile
That enchanted me, so the pause
That came before I spoke
Must have seemed strange to you,
And when I returned the compliment
So sweetly made, I still thought
Of the wistfulness of your smile.

So you like talking to people like me,
Friend with the wistful smile,
To foreign girls who are brown of skin
And have black kinky hair
And have strange black eyes.

You like to hear the tales I tell
Of a tropic Paradise,
Of sunkissed woods and mountains high
Of skies that are bluer than ever
Skies are blue in your nordic clime:
Of magic sunsets and marvellous seas,
Of waterfalls clattering down,
Stars so near, and the moon so large,
And fireflies, stars of the earth.

I like to listen to you,
Friend with the wistful smile.
It's not to hear of your great country
And tales of your marvellous land,
But to watch the wistful smile
That plays around your mouth,
The strange look in your eyes
And hear the calm sweet tone of your voice.

(*The Moth and The Star*, p. 16)

QUASHIE COMES TO LONDON

I gwine tell you 'bout de English
And I aint gwine tell no lie,
'Cause I come quite here to Englan'
Fe see wid me own eye.

I tell you fuss 'bout London town,
Hi man, it big fe true,
If you get lass as you often will
Is de Corpie put you troo.

An' talking 'bout de Bobbie dem,
Dem is nice as nice can be,
An' some o' dem is tall me boy
'Mos' like a coconut tree.

But dem nebber fas' wid you me frien'
Dem eben pass a fight,
An' fe see dem guide de traffic,
Man, it is a pretty sight.

I tink I love dem bes' of all
De people in dis town,
For dem seem to hab some life in dem
An' you nebber see dem frown.

I know you wan' fe hear jus' now
What I tink of dese white girls,
Well I tell you straight, dem smile 'pon me,
But I prefer black pearls!

You see dem always coated up,
It's no good fe go to a show
Fe see a crowd of lovely dames
All sitting in a row,

'Cause dem always hab a cloak
Or something fe kip dem warm,
So you can't admire dem in truth
And dat is jes' de harm.

An' dat takes me fe talk 'bout shows:
Now dem is someting gran'
An' if you nebber see one here
You jes' can't understand.

Dem hab de shows fe fit all taste
De highbrow and de low,
An' 'cording to de mood I hab
I choose de one fe go.

If I is feeling full o' pep
I choose variety,
Dem call dem all de nonstop show
An' tis dere you want to be.

Some of de numbers ain't so fine,
But dat you mus' expec'
But boy, I tell you, some again
Is surely full o' pep.

You hear some fun an' see some sights
Dem frown upon out dere,
But dough dem say dese people col'
De hot stuff gets de cheer.

An' sometimes jus when I feel gran'
Dere sitting all alone,
Dem play some tune dat takes me home
In sweet and soulful tone.

An' de tears dem well up in me eyes
An' I try fe brush dem 'way,
But me heart gets full and dough I try
Dem simply come fe stay.

For de orchestra is really gran'
I mean de bes' one dem,
For hot stuff gie me Harry Roy,
For sweet, Geraldo's men.

Sometimes de jazz gets in me bones
Me feet dem can't keep still,
I wants fe get right up and dance
But I use me good strong will.

I see some ob me own folks dem
In dese here music hall,
An' if you hear Paul Robeson sing
You feel you wan' fe bawl.

De folks dem love him here fe true,
An' all de coloured stars,
Dem love de darkies' tunes me frien'
An' try fe play guitars.

Dem love we songs, and I wan' tell you
Dat dough dem tink dem great,
Wid no glad darkies in de worl'
'Twould be a sad sad fate.

Now de oder times I go to plays
When I feel fe someting more
An' I hear English as she is spoke
An' it please me heart fe sure.

I don't go much to de Movie show
For I see so much back home,
Dem all is nice but jes' de same
Dem is but de ocean's foam.

But de organs dere delight me heart,
Dem stir me to me soul,
Dem tek me to dose pastures green
An' I hear Jordan roll.

An' dat minds me fe tell you now
'Bout de Parks dem in dis town,
Boy, if you wants something dat's fine
Jes' come along right down.

In spring you feel you heart astir
When you hear de birdies sing,
An' de flowers bloom and de leaves come out
An' de kids dance in a ring.

As quick as de sun can show his light
An' de air is a little warm,
Out to de Parks dem everywhere
You wan' see people swarm.

Dem sit like flies in Mango time
Under de lovely trees,
But all de same dem wear a coat
As if dem gwine fe freeze.

Man, some of de Parks is really fine,
Dem hab little lakes dem mek,
An' if you know fe row a boat
A nice one you can get.

If you walk de Parks on a real hot day
You'd a swear dat all de folk
Ain't got a blooming ting fe do
But sit in de sun fe joke.

For London town hab people man,
Dem jes' like gingy fly,
Dem say it's 'bout eight million
But a figure dat dem lie.

I mos' feget fe tell you now
About de place fe eat,
Massy massa, dere's a ting,
Now here's one big treat.

One day me walk upon de Stran'
Me see one place mark LYONS,
Me say Now Quashie, here's some fun
You better hol' you irons.

Me grab me umbrella real tight,
Yes man, me carry dat,
I step right in fe see de brutes
I fraid fe lif me hat.

But guess me what I fin' in dere
Not eben a lion's tail,
But a jazz ban' playing like it mad
An' folks eating grub wholesale.

I fin' a table to meself
An' I smile and look quite calm,
A little gal in black and white
Come speak to me wid charm.

She says "What can I get you sir?"
I says "Some ripe breadfruit,
Some fresh ackee and saltfish too
An' dumplins hot will suit."

She look pon me like say she lass,
A say "Why what's de row?"
She say "Sorry, but we have none sir"
An' I feel fe laugh somehow.

She gie me Menu fe go read,
You know I's good at dat,
But I say "no tanks, jes' bring me den
Some red herring an' sprat.

"An' anyting you hab fe food
Because I wan' a feed,"
You should see de dainty ting she bring,
It look like pigeon feed!

It's den I miss me home sweet home
Me good ole rice an' peas
An' I say I is a fool fe come
To dis lan' of starve an' sneeze.

But dis missive is too mighty long,
I will write more news nex time,
Me love fe all de gay spree boys
An' dat buxom gal o' mine.

It not gwine be anoder year
Before you see me face,
Dere's plenty dat is really nice
But I sick fe see white face.

(*The Moth and The Star*, pp. 17-21. Anthologised in the *Routledge Reader in Caribbean Literature* (1996))

HOME THOUGHTS

June is drawing near
And in my sun-kissed isle
The Poinciana with its flaming blossom
Casts its spell o'er all the land.
These mighty trees in regal robes
Now call the land to worship,
And the bees, hungry for hidden honey,
Swarm among its blossoms and buzz and buzz,
And the blossoms laugh and yield
Shedding their sweet perfume;
They make a crown of golden dust
To beautify the honeybee.

There on the hillside, 'mid a tuft
Of dark green trees, towers the Poinciana
Stretching its branches eagerly
To watch the children passing by.
I see a tree I used to love
Whose red and golden glory
Has thrilled my soul with wonder;
O, I remember that glad June,
So long ago it seems,
'Twas Harvest in the Village Church
And the merry school children
Cut great branches of Poinciana
And made a radiant glory of the Church.

June comes again and Poinciana trees
Now blossom in my sunkissed isle
And I am here in London, and the flowers
Of dainty shades and delicate perfumes
Stir my heart and wake my love,
But it is to the flaming glory
Of Poinciana trees in fair Jamaica

That my lone heart is homing.
I might sing of fragrant Myrtle blossoms
Whiter than snow and sweeter than honey,
Of pink and white June roses,
Of Jessamines, Hibiscus, Begonias,
Of Bougainvillea and Cassia,
But the Flaming Poinciana
Calls to me across the distance
Calling, calling me home.

O pride and glory of our tropic Isle,
As thy red and golden petals
Drip blood drops on the sod
That thou mayst bring forth
Mighty pods of fertile seed,
So children of your tropic land
With broken hearts that bleed
In foreign lands afar
Strain every nerve to bring forth
Fruit that may enrich the race
And are anew inspired
With hope and loyal longing –
Hope that thy red and golden banners
Now unfurled through all the land
May call men's hearts
To bow at Beauty's shrine –
And loyal longing that awakes
And claims the best thy sons and daughters give.

O Fair Jamaica! my thoughts go home to you,
In love and loyalty I shall for aye be true.

(*The Moth and the Star*, pp. 22-3. A revised version 'Home Thoughts in
June' appears in *Towards the Stars* (pp. 20-1). This version begins with
the third stanza of the original poem and ends before the final couplet).

NOSTALGIA

I will arise and go again to my fair Tropic Isle
And sit beneath the palm trees that there forever smile,

I must leave this lovely country for one that's lovelier far,
I would leave the land of glow-worms and seek again the star.

The purple hills are calling and the orange is in bloom,
The dew is on the Myrtle and the violets fade so soon.

The lovely Lignum Vitae trees are basking in the sun,
They are whispering and wondering just when once more I'll come

To lie beneath the shade and watch the colours of the sea
And dream of all the bygone days and days that are to be.

My loving friends with eager eyes are waiting for the day
When I'll come and hold their hands and ever with them stay.

Oh, I'll arise and go again to my fair Tropic Isle
For I hear voices calling and I'm so sad meanwhile.

(*The Moth and The Star*, p. 24)

HEARTBREAK COTTAGES

Here on the fringe of our fair Southern Coast,
In an isle of whose beauty multitudes boast
Is scenery divine that is ne'er told in rhyme
And a glory effaced not by time.

But Nature's exquisite landscape has blots;
On the peasant's miniature housing plots
Are heartbreak cottages never designed
Where workers rest from a day's hard grind.

Some homes are of zinc and others of thatch,
Some that nothing on earth can match;
They are patched and mended, unfit for the eyes
Of the poorest of poor living under the skies.

O you that live in homes that are grand –
How can you permit this disgrace in the land?
Go teach your brothers the joys of a home,
Go help them to build where in darkness they roam.

Heartbreak cottages must go in the sand,
Pride of race sun cots must stand in our land.
O my people, of careless content beware;
There's beauty oft found in poverty's care.

O my people, build hearts that are true to the core,
Remember your children who play round your door;
Their innocence pity; they all have a dream –
O save them from blindness, your honour redeem.

(*The Moth and The Star*, p. 28)

DARLINGFORD

Blazing tropical sunshine
On a hard, white, dusty road
That curves round and round
Following the scraggy coastline;
Coconut trees fringing the coast,
Thousands and thousands
Of beautiful coconut trees,
Their green and brown arms
Reaching out in all directions –
Reaching up to high heaven
And sparkling in the sunshine.
Sea coast, rocky sea coast
Rocky palm fringed coastline;
Brown-black rocks,
White sea-foam spraying the rocks;
Waves, sparkling waves
Dancing merrily with the breeze;
The incessant song
Of the mighty sea.
A white sail – far out
Far, far out at sea
A tiny sailing boat –
White sails all glittering
Flirting with the bright rays
Of the soon setting sun,
Trying to escape their kisses,
In vain – and the jealous winds
Waft her on, on, out to sea
Till sunset, then weary
Of their battle with the sun
The tired winds
Fold themselves to sleep
And the noble craft
No longer idolised

By her two violent lovers
Drifts slowly into port
In the pale moonlight;
Gone are the violent caresses
Of the sun and restless winds –
She nestles in the cool embrace
Of quiet waves
And tender moonlight.
Southern silvery moonlight
Shining from a pale heaven
Upon a hard, white, dusty road
That curves round and round
Following the craggy coastline
Of Jamaica's southern shores.

(*The Moth and The Star*, pp. 29-30, *Towards the Stars*, p. 8-10.
Anthologised in *Treasury of Jamaican Poetry*, edited by J.E. Clare
McFarlane (University of London Press Ltd, 1949), pp. 44-5 and
Caribbean Voices: An Anthology of West Indian Poetry: volume 1 edited by
John Figueroa (London: Evans Brothers Ltd, 1966), pp. 32-3)

TO THE HIBISCUS

Fair Hibiscus oft you linger
In the gardens of the poor
Bringing joy and cheer and brightness
To the peasant's lowly door.

There thy blossoms bloom in splendour
Telling all that pass you by
That earth's beauty and earth's gladness
To the poorest heart is nigh.

Fair Hibiscus, thou art frailer
Than the blooms of roses rare,
Picked and prisoned fast thou diest,
Free, thou growest without care.

Fairest cup of reddest radiance
Joy thou bringest to my heart,
Teach me thine own joyful message
That I may such cheer impart.

(*The Moth and The Star*, p. 35, *Towards the Stars*, p. 12)

WINGED ANTS

Winged ant
The rains have come
And your house of wood
Is watersoaked and cold
So you and your friends
Have come to my house.
I am sorry you thought fit
To fly on my paper
To see what I had written
Because a sudden impulse,
An irresistible desire
Came over me, I had to find
How many wings you had
Folded into one
As you crawled about
On my white sheet of paper;
I put my finger
On your frail gossamer wings
And suddenly you walked away
Leaving your precious wings
Under my fingertips.
Now I repent in grief
For, little creature
You will fly no more
And now I feel your woe;
Has not life's hard caress
Forced from me glad wings
That bore me to the stars
When first I saw the wonder
And beauty of the world?
Little winged ant,
Forgive my erring hands,
I should have known that wings
Are frail and delicate unearthly things.

(*The Moth and The Star*, p. 36, *Towards the Stars*, p. 13)

MY BELOVED

I will make thee my Beloved,
I will sing to thee
Songs that are sweet;
I will send to thee
Thoughts that are beautiful.
I will give to thee
Smiles that are tender;
I will smooth for thee
Paths that are rough;
I will paint for thee
Exquisite pictures;
I will play to thee
Music divine;
I will comfort thee
When thou art weary;
I will cheer you
When thou art sad.
I will be near thee
When thou art lonely;
I will send to thee
Sweet dreams at night time;
I will make for thee
Days of delight.
And all —
And more than all —
Thou askest,
I will do for thee —
I will make thee my Beloved.

(*The Moth and the Star*, p. 41, *Towards the Stars*, pp. 22-3)

LOVE SONGS

I am a woman
So I sing of Love,
I sing of Love
Because I am a woman;
Nay, more than this,
Because Love lingers not
But leaves me desolate
I sing of Love
To charm her back
To me.
But will she hear my songs?
Nay, that she will not,
She is deaf and blind,
She will not hear,
She will not see,
She will not come to me.
E'en so, let her pass on,
She knows I will no more
Suffer love's pain,
And yet,
I am a woman
So I sing of Love,
I sing of Love
Because I am a woman.

(*The Moth and the Star*, p. 42, *Towards the Stars*, pp. 27-8)

THE HEART'S CUNNING

Heart of mine, why do you beat so fast?
Why do you murmur so?
I will not listen,
I will not hear you,
I will not understand.
I am deaf to your pleadings,
The door is shut,
The door is locked,
The golden key
Lies somewhere beneath the sea.

Heart of mine, I cannot answer make,
I have no eyes to search the sands,
There is no other key will do,
I am wise, and you are foolish,
You would make a fool of me,
You bid me use my magic power
You cast a spell about me,
And remind me of this power.
Once – in days long past
You pleaded – you gave promise,
But now it is in vain,
In vain you plead.

For you would lead me on
And lose my soul
In sightless ecstasy;
I will have none of you.
Let me sleep in peace,
Let me not listless lie
Awake at nights
And count the hours.
Lead me not forth again
Up to the high mountains

Only to send me down
Into the dreary, dismal depths.

Time I have not, and wish no more.
I do not desire your guidance,
I cannot trust you,
No more will I answer you,
Nor bow to you in awe.
Silence! Speak not, stir not,
Murmur not, plead not –
I tell you it is vain.
If life can give some joy
It is enough – so I can live,
But with your charméd pain
I cannot breathe – Silence I pray
I am too young to die.

(*The Moth and The Star*, pp. 43-4)

NIGHTFALL

How tender the heart grows
  At the twilight hour,
More sweet seems the perfume
  Of the sunless flower.

Come quickly, wings of night,
  The twilight hurts too deep;
Let darkness wrap the world around,
  My pain will go to sleep.

(*The Moth and the Star*, p. 53, *Towards the Stars*, p. 23. Anthologised in *The Poetry of the Negro 1746-1949* edited by Langston Hughes and Arna Bontemps (New York: Doubleday & Company, Inc. 1949), p. 325 and in the unpublished *The Anthology of Poetry of the West Indies*, chosen and edited by W. Adolphe Roberts and Wycliffe Bennett, 1953.)

MY NEED

Speak to me –
For when you speak
I am strong and well and awake.

Smile on me –
For when you smile
I am thankful that I am alive.

Hold my hands –
For at your touch
The world becomes a magic land.

Be near to me –
For at your side
I find my best and truest self.

Live on forever
That I may live
And love that spirit which thou art;

But love me not
Lest naught be left
In life worth my desire.

(*The Moth and the Star*, p. 53, *Towards the Stars*, p. 23)

THE IMPOSSIBLE

You ask me just to be a little wise,
To half subdue the ardour in my eyes,
To find some unseen power that can restrain
The heated blood that rushes to my brain.

Ask then the wild wind on its furious course
To half subdue its mighty unspent force,
And ask the troubled sea that she no more
Will dash her waves against the placid shore.

Ask of the fire that's blazing ever higher
Of its consuming appetite to tire,
And ask the sun that moves towards the west
To stay its course, subdue its heat and rest:

Ask on, your chiding is so sweet to me
I have no wish to seek for clemency.

(*The Moth and the Star*, p. 55, *Towards the Stars*, p. 24)

REASONING

There is no love in your eyes
I would have seen it,
There is no love in your touch,
I would have felt it,
There is no love in your heart
I would have known it.

There is love in my eyes
You have seen it,
There is love in my touch
You have felt it,
There is love in my heart
You know it.

It is well that this should be:
I will love on
And you remain unmoved;
Your coldness will feed my fire
For love reciprocated burns away
And only the ashes
Of dead desire remain.

(The Moth and the Star, p. 57)

CONFESSION

I regret nothing –
I have lived
I have loved
I have known laughter
And dance and song,
I have wept,
I have sighed
I have prayed,
I have soared
On fleecy clouds
To the gates
Of heaven,
I have sunk
Deep down
In the pit
Of hell.

I have heard
Laughter
Of little children
At dawn,
I have seen
Exquisite sunsets,
I have found
Comfort
With my friends
And grief
With my foes,
I have pressed
Little white daisies
To my lips.

I know
The breath

Of the tulip
And jessamine,
I have seen
Daffodils in Spring
Roses in June
And the Poinciana
Dripping blood.
I have seen
Bright stars
Leap adown heaven
At the call of some earth flower;
I have been close
To death
And watched him
At work.
I have heard music
That raised
My soul
To worlds unknown,
I have danced
With fairies
On moonswept lawns,
I have watched
with mermaids
Under the sea
At Neptune's Court.

I have been part
Of sea and air and sky,
Of all sorrows
That have been
And are to be,
All joys of earth,
All evil and all good.

I have tried
To bring joy
To sad hearts –
Maybe I have sent
Sorrow to some heart,
If that be so
In sorrow I repent;
That, I desired not.

But so God bless me,
I have no regrets – .
And should death
Come close
Beside me now
And bid me follow,
Smiling still,
Would I go,
For though I leave
Some friends
On earth,
I go
I know not where
To join those
My beloved ones
Who wait for me.
Why should I
Sorrowing go?
Have I not lived?

(*The Moth and The Star*, p. 63)

THE BANJO BOY

Black boy,
How you play that banjo!
Gee – it goes right to my toes,
I could dance all night
And through the day again.
How your face beams.
Do you love it?
I'll say you do.

Where did you get that rhythm?
That swing and that motion,
That bubbling laughter
With which you punctuate
Your songs? I have it too,
I can feel it going through me,
But I can't express like you do.

You know it's good to be alive,
Don't you, as long as the sun shines
And the banjo is in your hands?
Maybe you are hungry,
Maybe your shirt is going,
Maybe you are not worth a gill,
But what do you care?

There's your banjo, the boys come
And sing and hum and dance
Round you – they share in your joy,
They respond to your songs –
Those banjo songs that call me.

(*The Moth and The Star*, p. 68)

THE STONE BREAKERS

"Liza me chile, I's really tired
Fe broke dem stone,
Me han' hat me,
Me back hat me,
Me foot hat me,
An' Lard, de sun a blin' me."

"No so, Cousin Mary, an' den
De big backra car dem
A lik up de dus' in a we face.
Me Massa Jesus knows it,
I's weary of dis wol' –

"But whey fe do, Cousin Mary,
Me haf fe buy frack fe de pickney dem,
Ebry day dem hab fe feed.
Dem wot'less pupa tan roun' de bar
A trow dice all de day –
De groun' is dat dry,
Not a ting will grow –
Massy Lard, dis life is hard.
An' so – dough de work is hard
I will has to work fe pittance
Till de good Lard call me."

"Liza me chile, I's really tired
But wha fe do – we mus' brok de stone
Dough me han' dem hat me
Me back it hat me,
Me foot dem hat me
And de sun it blin' me –
Well – de good Lard knows
All about we sorrows."

(*The Moth and The Star*, p. 70)

MY PHILOSOPHY

(As expounded by a Market Woman).

(Market woman walking quickly ahead of her friend. She carries a huge basket on her head. She swings both hands violently as she addresses the friend close behind her without turning):

> "You can tan up talk wid him,
> If you and him is companion
> Me and him is no companion."

(Second market woman following quickly at her heels):

> "Me and him is companion, yes
> Me and him is companion
> Me and all de wide worl' is companion
> For dere is nobody better dan me
> And I is not better dan nobody."

(*The Moth and The Star*, p. 71)

"BLACK IS FANCY"

I am very black,
I look in the mirror,
My eyes are bright,
And my teeth,
They are very white.

There is a picture in my room,
It is a picture
Of a beautiful white lady,
I used to think her sweet,
But now I think
She lacks something.

I used to feel
I was so ugly
Because I am black,
But now I am glad I am black,
There is something about me
That has a dash in it
Especially when I put on
My bandana.

Since Aunt Liza gave me
This nice looking glass
I begin to be real proud
Of my own self.
I think I will take down
This white lady's picture,
It used to make me ashamed,
And all black folk
Seemed ugly.

But I don't know,
This white lady is sweet,
But she is too white,
Besides, she is not my friend,
She is my mistress.
I think she is too white.
Maybe I will be more proud
Of my black skin, if I don't see her,
I will remove her picture.

My John told me I was sweet,
I did not believe him,
Thought he would go mooning around
Some whitewash girl,
But maybe he means it,
For I am not so dull,
Yes, I am sure he loves me
His black ivory girl,
And I love him
For he is young, and strong and black.

(*The Moth and The Star*, pp. 75-6)

GETTIN' DE SPIRIT

Lord gie you chile de spirit
Let her shout
Lord gie your chile de power
An' let her pray –
Hallelujah – Amen –
Shout sister – shout –
God is sen' you His spirit
Shout – sister – shout.

Shout sister – shout –
Hallelujah – Amen.
Can't you feel de spirit
Shout sister – shout
Hallelujah – Amen.

Join de chorus,
We feel it flowing o'er us –
You is no chile of satan
So get de spirit
And shout – sister – shout –
Hallelujah – Amen –
Shout – Sister – Shout!

(*The Moth and The Star*, p. 76. Also anthologised in the *Penguin Book of Caribbean Verse* (1986) edited by Paula Burnett, p. 160 and in the 2005 *Modern Women Poets* edited by Deryn Rees-Jones (Newcastle: Bloodaxe Books), p. 85-6)

LITTLE BOYS

Why should they tease me, Mother
Because my skin is black?
I go to school with white boys
Some of them are gentle to me
But some of them are so rude
They try to hurt me when we play.

Why do they call me "nigger",
And laugh at me, Mother?
Does it matter that my skin is black
And theirs is white?
Your skin is black, Mother,
But you are beautiful,
And I love you.

Because they despise me, Mother,
I work so hard, so hard,
For I must be top of the class
So tho' they may not like my skin
They will see that I work hard
That I am honest and gentle and kind;
But tell me, Mother darling,
Didn't God make all little boys?

[*The Moth and The Star*, p.78]

WINIFRED HOLTBY

They do but err who tell me thou art dead
And that thy dwelling lies beyond the skies,
How can the Spring return if thou are fled
And speedwells bloom that mirror'd thy soft eyes?

Thy freshness was the envy of the Spring,
Thine was the joy of summer's radiant noon,
Of thy enchanting ways did songbirds sing
And can it be that thou art gone so soon?

O valiant woman, author, speaker, friend,
With sympathies as wide as they were true;
Thy heart was like a fount where all might bend
To drink, and find their faith in life anew:

Now well might time itself live but a day
Did radiant souls remain enthralled in clay.

(*The Moth and The Star*, p. 79, *Towards the Stars*, pp. 46-7)

TO THE I.A.W.S.E.C.

Women of England who in freedom's name
Work with courageous women of all lands,
For women's rights, yet not for women's fame,
I greet you, and to you stretch friendly hands.
In your inspiring work I had my part
For you were more than passing kind to me,
In Istanbul they took me to their heart
Where women of far lands met glad and free.
What courage have fair England's women shown
In public life and in the quiet home,
What bitter struggles have their spirit known
So that just rights to womanhood should come:
For lands can only reach the greater good
When noble thoughts inspire sweet womanhood.

*

(*The Moth and The Star*, p. 80, *Towards the Stars*, p. 47)

TO JOE AND BEN

*(Brutally murdered in April 1937 at Addis Abbaba by
the Italians)*

As David and Jonathan
So you seemed to me
In your love and devotion
One for the other.

They sent you forth
From "England's pleasant land",
Home of your fond adoption,
Of early boyhood's years –
They sent you forth
To the battle's front
To fight for a country
Yours, and yet not yours
By unfamiliarity.

I wept for you
As you two gallant sons
Went forth
From the brightness
Of an English summer
To die
On the mountain heights
Of Ethiopia.
I saw the tears
In your bright eyes
As you stood
Side by side
As ever you had stood –
I felt the swell of your throat
As bravely smiling
You bade farewell.

Forth you went
To your homeland
Gallant sons
Of Ethiopia
So young
And so beautiful
In your
Youthful splendour.
There were not enough
Of Ethiopia's youth
To dye her fields
Blood red
So you went forth;
But Nature cherished you,
Her darlings,
Grown in another clime,
Nurtured in her tongue,
Bred in her customs;
You were too young
And brave
And gentle
And so death
Passed you by.
Bombs rained
From hell's corsairs
Upon you
But you were still
Unscathed.
Conquered your land
But still
With the unconquered
Band of gallant warriors
You stood
Side by side,
In danger undivided.

One more gallant task,
One desperate rush
To free the land
That gave you birth
From savagery's dark reign
And then –
Death met you,
Called you by name,
Not in the midst of battle,
Not hewn down
In heated blood
But after hellish tortures
You were murdered
In cold blood
As traitors
To the land
For which you died.
Jonathan and Benjamin
Two gallant sons
Of Ethiopia
Tender and young
And fair as women
Lay cold and dead
Side by side.
As they had lived
In love together
Even in death
They were undivided,
Even the death
Of traitors.

God, I know
That these thine own
And thousands more
Cut down in youth
And beauty

Are not dead,
They live forever
In our hearts
And their spirits
To earth will come
Again in other form
That they may live
For that high destiny
Which brought them
Earthwards.

God in heaven,
This hate and greed
That brings forth war –
When shall it cease?
Dost thou unmoved
Watch the destinies
Of man
Thy own creation?

(*The Moth and The Star*, pp. 81-3)

AT THE PRISON GATES

They marched
To the prison walls and knocked at the gates,
And when he who was director came forth
They spoke and said unto him
"We are hungry, we need food for our bodies,
We would join your band of prisoners
And work, so be that we are fed.
We are men, we need work, we need food.
Our wives and sweethearts live in poverty,
We have nothing to take to them;
We are strong – we would work – but
No man will employ us."

And he the director spake unto them
Words that could not comfort,
Words that could not feed,
Words that could not give hope,
Yet they were kind words;
And the sorrowful army
Of Kingston's unemployed marched on –
On with their empty stomachs,
Their empty pockets,
With no hope in their hearts,
With no comfort in their souls.

And I looked,
And behold I saw numerous men,
Wealthy, overfed, over-indulged –
And when they heard this
Their hearts smote them
And some of these men said,
"Are not these men our brothers?"
And others said – "Indeed they are not –
They are worthless creatures who will not work."
And one said, "But in other lands,

There are unemployment funds."
And some said, "Let us arise
And pool ten thousand pounds,
And let us give these men land
And money to assist them."
And another said – "Nay, let us build us
Great factories and use our raw materials
So we can provide work for them,
For they are men."

And so they talked the while
Their conscience smote them,
And they drank together and
Went away happy for they pledged no wealth
To be used so that no more
Weary and hungry marchers
Would walk to the prison gates
Of Kingston and desire to enter
So they might be fed.

And so all through the night and day
I see the weary and hungry
Crowds – marching – every day
More hungry – every day more sad;
And I hear a great stir of voices
Among those who rule the land
In politics and those who rule in gold;
But the tramp of the weary feet still sound.
They who are free men march on
To seek the bondage from which
Others died to free them –
That they might have food.
On they march – must they march on
Forever?

(*The Moth and The Star*, pp. 85-6)

CINEMA EYES

Don't want you to go to the Cinema –
Yes, I know you are eighteen,
I know your friends go,
I know you want to go.

I used to go to the Cinema
To see beautiful white faces.
How I worshipped them!
How beautiful they seemed –
I grew up with a cinema mind.

My ideal man would be a Cinema type –
No kinky haired man for me,
No black face, no black children for me.
I would take care
Not to get sun burnt,
To care my half Indian hair
To look like my cinema stars.

I saw no beauty in black faces,
The tender light and beauty
Of their eyes I did not see;
The smoothness of their skin,
The mellow music of their voice,
The stateliness of their walk,
The tenderness of their hearts
No, they were black
And therefore had no virtue.

A handsome youth came
To woo me at twenty;
I did not think him handsome then –
He was black and not my fancy.
I turned my back on him –

My instinct told me he was good and true,
My reason told me he was black
I turned my back on him.

Another came to woo me –
How fair he was! How like
My ideal built up in my heart –
I gave to him my heart,
My life, my soul, my all;
And how in hell he tortured me,
My dream lover – my husband –
Then you were born,
But I remained disconsolate.

He too saw no beauty in black faces,
You came dark like your grandmother;
He was peeved. I thought
You just a little like
My first handsome suitor
Who so long had gone away; –
He would have been more kind –
More tender – So I thought aloud
One day and he o'erheard me.

Soon this black god came from far
And called to greet me.
My husband, in fury and in drink,
Watched us as we talked –
And as he rose to go
Followed him calmly out,
And shot him, ere he reached the gate.
Another bullet sound,
And he too was gone;
And we were left alone.

I know that love
Laughs at barriers,
Of race and creed and colour.
But I know that black folk
Fed on movie lore
Lose pride of race.
I would not have you so.

Come, I will let you go
When black beauties
Are chosen for the screen;
That you may know
Your own sweet beauty
And not the white loveliness
Of others for envy.

(*The Moth and the Star*, pp. 87-8. Anthologised in the *Routledge Reader in Caribbean Literature* (1996), pp. 138-40.)

GOING TO MARKET

Old lady
You dig in the fields
All day long,
Are you not weary
Does your head not ache?

How hot are the sun's rays,
How strong is the glare,
How the heat comes up
From the parched land
And down from the high heavens.

I know it is Friday
And you are digging
To find food
To take to market.
Are you not afraid
To travel so far
On the long hot
And dreary roads?

I know you will find
A truck or a tram at last,
But by then, your poor naked feet
Will be sore and weary.
And then perhaps
The market is bad
And you cannot afford
The food and print
You meant to buy.

Old lady, life is hard for you
And yet you smile sweetly
When you speak to me,

And you talk gaily
With others.
Old Lady, I am sorry
The sun beats down
So relentlessly on you
As you journey.

Old lady, I love you
For the courage you bring
To life – for your goodness
Of heart and your hope
Of a heaven
Where there are no hot fields
And hotter highways –
Where the streets
Are paved with gold,
And even the Great God Himself
Will wipe all tears
From your eyes.

(*The Moth and The Star*, pp. 89-90)

KINKY HAIR BLUES

Gwine find a beauty shop
Cause I ain't a belle.
Gwine find a beauty shop
Cause I ain't a lovely belle.
The boys pass me by,
They say I's not so swell.

See older young gals
So slick and smart.
See those oder young gals
So slick and smart.
I jes gwine die on de shelf
If I don't mek a start.

I hate dat ironed hair
And dat bleaching skin.
Hate dat ironed hair
And dat bleaching skin.
But I'll be all alone
If I don't fall in.

Lord 'tis you did gie me
All dis kinky hair.
'Tis you did gie me
All dis kinky hair,
And I don't envy gals
What got dose locks so fair.

I like me black face
And me kinky hair.
I like me black face
And me kinky hair.
But nobody loves dem,
I jes don't tink it's fair.

Now I's gwine press me hair
And bleach me skin.
I's gwine press me hair
And bleach me skin.
What won't a gal do
Some kind a man to win.

(*The Moth and The Star*, p. 91. Anthologised in the *Penguin Book of Caribbean Verse* (1986), p.158-9; the *Routledge Reader in Caribbean Literature* (1996), pp. 137-8, and in the *2005 Modern Women Poets* (Newcastle: Bloodaxe Books), pp. 86-7))

BLACK BURDEN

I am black
And so I must be
More clever than white folk,
More wise than white folk,
More discreet than white folk,
More courageous than white folk.

I am black,
And I have got to travel
Even farther than white folk,
For time moves on –
I must not laugh too much,
They say black folk can only laugh,
I must not weep too much,
They say black folk weep always
I must not pray too much
They say black folk can only pray.

I am black,
What a burden lies
Upon my heart –
For I would see
All my race
Holding hands
In the world circle.

Black girl – what a burden –
But your shoulders
Are broad
Black girl – what a burden –
But your courage is strong –
Black girl your burden

Will fall from your shoulders
For there is love
In your soul
And a song
In your heart.

(*The Moth and The Star*, p. 93, *Towards the Stars*, p. 93)

CANEFIELD BLUES

Down in de canefield
Wid my Mandy sweet.
Down in de canefield
Wid my Mandy sweet,
When she gives a groan
And tumble cross me feet.

Bury me Mandy,
By de garden gate,
Bury me Mandy
By de garden gate,
Now dere's noting lef' for me,
What a cruel fate.

Mandy was de bes' gal
In all de lan'.
Mandy was de bes' gal
In all de lan';
But de sun come tek her
Right out a me han'.

I don't nebber will see
Anoder gal like she.
I don't nebber will see
Anoder gal like she;
Because my Mandy
Was eber sweet to me.

(*The Moth and The Star*, p. 94)

TO CONNIE

Connie gal, Connie gal,
Tell me where you been,
De way you treat a good man
It really is a sin.

See how Marty beat him gal
Gwine do dat to you,
You's a double crossing pal
Hat me heart fe true.

Connie gal, Connie gal,
Don't you raise me ire,
Go back to you Aunt Sal
If you make me tire.

Can't you see I loves you
Connie, me sweetheart?
Don't you know I need you
Why you break me heart?

(*The Moth and The Star*, p. 96)

LONESOME BLUES

I got dose lonesome blues
O what can I do?
I got does lonesome blues,
O what can I do?
I must just lay me down
And weep de whole night thro'.

Nobody cares
If I don't come home,
Nobody cares
If I don't come home,
What's de good o' dis life
Jes as well I roam.

It's kinda hard
Being a lonesome gal,
It's kinda hard
Being a lonesome gal,
But I bet it's worse
Wid a no good pal.

(*The Moth and The Star*, p. 96)

BROWN BABY BLUES

I got a brown baby
Sweet as she can be.
I got a brown baby
Sweet as she can be.
But she ain't got no papa,
Cause he's gone to sea.

I love me baby
But she don't got no name.
I love me baby
She don't got no name.
Well wha' fe do,
Dat is not her shame.

Maybe she'll ask me
Why I is so black,
Maybe she'll ask me
Why I is so black,
An' she's so brown;
Lord send her papa back.

My sweet brown baby
Don't you cry.
My sweet brown baby
Don't you cry.
Your mamma does love you
And you colour is high.

(*The Moth and The Star*, p. 97. Also anthologised in the *Penguin Book of Caribbean Verse,* (1986), p. 159)

FOREIGN

He was just an old man
In shabby shirt and shabbier trousers;
I did not see him at first
It was after I took off my shoes
And wading and splashing
The waves up with my feet
That I saw him stroll along
And lie comfortably on the grass,
His head supported by one arm.
He looked at me, then conversed
With two men who sat on the bench;
They were ordinary men
Much better dressed than he was.

When I grew tired of sporting
With the restless waves
And strutting about on the pebbles
I returned and put on my shoes.
I walked lightheartedly along the beach,
Someone spoke to me,
It was the shabby old man.
I turned to hear him:
"Missus, if you find some gold
In de san' will you give me some?"
He said and smiled a smile
That beamed all over his lined face.
"Of course I will," I replied,
And returned his pleasant smile.
From that moment we were friends.

I strolled along and lay on a bench
Hard by. It was late afternoon, the sun,
Weary of its heat had gentle grown
And so I lay beneath his kind caress.

I closed my eyes, and opened them
Again and once again to make full sure
That I was not asleep and in a dream –
The sea – the shadows on the mountain –
The boat with sails outspread
Wafted along the mighty seas –
The palms swaying against
The radiant skies – Then I would close
Them fast when reassured and quite content.

The sound of children's voices
Roused me. I sat up, unable
To resist the sound of child laughter.
Alas, they had moved on. My old friend
Was sitting on the ground quite near
Weeding bunches of grass with both hands.
Near him stood his mule and cart,
"Here pretty fe true ma'am," he said
As his keen eyes scanned the horizon,
"But tings is bad, foreign better,
Things will never better here, never" –
And then finding me a ready listener
He told me many tales – the while
He drew the grass to make hay for his mule.

"I have been in foreign – I was wid
De Contingent dat go to Halifax ma'am –
Dere I get fross bitten – it was so cold.
Egypt and France and Italy I see –
In foreign dey say we speak too much
Of King, dat's why we so poor.
We mus speak of President we chose ourself
An' if he don't suit we throw him out.
In foreign I never see people go like we –
Tear pants and soil shirt. In foreign
Dey not so poor as we – and talking

'Bout eating – in foreign wit de army
How we eat! Not like the starvation
Little food we eat here from day to day
Dat mek us weak and sick –
We eat plenty food – so if one day
Rations short and we have only biscuit,
We don't sick, for we strong on 'count
Of plenty food oder times.

"Did you know 'bout de goat in de Army?
It come from foreign you know –
Dat place where Marcus Garvey was going –
Africa – yes Africa – de goat up
At Camp – and de Colonel tek him –
Oh him wise more dan some man.
If de goat smell water and don't drink,
Don't you touch it – it poison.
Don't you touch anything dat goat refuse.
And to see him drill – him understand
Every command de Colonel give – Oh you
Can't think ma'am how wonderful
Dat goat is.

"See dis mark in my elbow ma'am –
A bullet shot right through it
And kill a man behind me
And dat time I was not fraid –
Dose times we men not fraid –
Dey give us tings to drink dat
Give us spirit – but ma'am –
When we 'fraid is when de bombs
Explode – Lord help us, what a roar
And how it tear de earth and root
Up de biggest trees!
Tings tek long fe do here.
In foreign in de Army dem hab

Machine dat dig up a whole
Mountain and in few minutes
One powerful machine
Pick up earth and tree and rock and pitch dem 'way.

"Foreign is nice but here it hard –
Here dey pay servant three shillings a week –
Wha' dat can buy? It can't
Pay rent – it can't buy frock
It can't buy shoes it can't buy stocking
It can't buy nothing – is what them to do?
Foreign better, – dem pay plenty more –
Even Cuba better dan us here.
Here if you talk you min' dem
Prison you. You know ma'am
Kaiser was good fighter and if
Englan' one did fight Kaiser, Kaiser
Would win – Kaiser wise him build
Under worl' town so when bomb
Drop – de earth tear, but in de
Undergroun' town all is safe –
I hear England doing dat now.

"You been foreign ma'am?
You tink here better dan
Foreign? All it hab is poverty
But noting more,
And you see how people fas'
Into one anoder business here ma'am –
Foreign you can't do dat.
If you interfere, no quarrel, no talk,
You see like I sitting here ma'am
And I did fas' wid a man,
I don't hear no soun', but from
Where him stan' him just send
A bullet through me – not a sound

But a lay stiff dead. In foreign
Dem don't play and quarrel, quarrel –
Dem talk wid bullet."

At this point
Came a family and joined our
Group – My friend became silent
And continued his weeding –
I rose – the sun was very near setting
And the wind was a little cold.
I said good-bye to the kind old man
And he said he hoped he would
See me again. I too hoped so.
He was a grand old man.
He loved to tell his tales of "foreign"
And how I loved to hear them.

(*The Moth and The Star*, pp. 99-102)

UNPUBLISHED C 1944

PARIS AND LONDON

The women in Paris are lovely to see
Though they work for their men in sincerity,
They dress with great care, look charming and neat
No trousers and uniforms worn on the street.

The women in London efficient and tough
In their uniforms they are ready and rough,
Severe and well meaning they want all to see
They're doing their bit conscientiously.

Now London I love, Paris I adore.
London gives me much, but Paris gives more.
I like my women efficient and brave
But the feminine dame fairly makes me her slave.

*Note. This unpublished poem is held in the Una Marson Papers, Box MS 1994C, at the National Library of Jamaica.

TOWARDS THE STARS

"THEY ALSO SERVE"

They were just a dozen privates
With an hour or two to spare,
They lunched on the grub in the canteen
And they didn't seem to care

About war or hate or women,
About guns and bombs and blast,
Nor for that a commission
Or how long the war might last.

They didn't belong to the Grenadier Guards
Or some far-famed highland clan,
They were simply men of the Pioneer Corps
In the lovely Isle of Man.

And what did they do – on this April day,
These lads in brown with an hour to spare? –
They came strolling down to the warm seafront
Along the beach as far as they dare.

The sun was hot, and the tide coming in,
So they did what I had been longing to do –
They took off their boots and wandered out
To meet the waves – for a dance or two.

Not much glamour about it all,
But the Army boots slog on just the same –
The cool of the sand and sea was a call,
And to kiss their feet the wild waves came.

(*Towards the Stars*, p. 18)

163

INTERLUDE

Still is the night,
The great city sleeps
Wrapped in her black mantle;
The stars keep vigil
And sentries watch
Over a land
Waiting in hushed horror.

Suddenly, out of stillness,
Out of silent night,
Down from the infected heights
May come death and desolation.
Meanwhile, silence,
A wakeful sleeping,
And the vigil
Of stars
And sentries.

(*Towards the Stars*, p. 43)

THE TEST

The test of true culture
Is the ability
To move among men,
East or West,
North or South,
With ease and confidence,
Radiating the pure light
Of a kindly humanity.

(*Towards the Stars*, p. 43)

POLITENESS

They tell us
That our skin is black
But our hearts are white.

We tell them
That their skin is white
But their hearts are black.

(*Towards the Stars*, p. 44. Also anthologised in the *Penguin Book of Caribbean Verse* (1986), p.160.)

IN THE DARKNESS

Groping amid the darkness
In the streets of a city
Once gay with myriad lights
Is a mysterious sensation.
At first I felt afraid,
Then strangely mystified,
And, without thinking,
Almost instinctively
I asked God to take my hand.

(Towards the Stars, p. 45)

FROZEN

Winter 1941

Europe is frozen.
It is too cold for birds to sing,
For children to make snowmen,
For rivers to splash and sparkle,
For lovers to loiter in the snowlight.

The heart of humanity is frozen.
It is too cold for Poets to sing.

(*Towards the Stars*, p. 45)

DAWN

No more do men
Climb up to lofty heights
To greet the dawn
And chant hymns of praise
To the Eternal
Sun God.

Instead they fly
Like bats and owls
That seek their prey
In darkness –
And in the dawn
They, returning
With the Sun's return,
Cast gloomy shadows
On his radiant face
And dull the splendour
That should gild the dawn.

(Towards the Stars, p. 51)

UNPUBLISHED LATER POEMS

EMERGENCE

Out of the darkness
   came the light;
Out of the night
   the day:
Through the dark clouds
   the sunlight streamed
And winter turned
   to Spring.

Out of the rain –
   a nightingale
Out of the storm
   a rainbow came:
Up through the frost
   a crocus bloom'd
Down from the ice
   a streamlet flowed.

Out of the silence
   children's laughter;
Out of the clay
   a beauteous thing:
On thorny briars
   a budding rose;
From the dead seed
   a fresh green stalk.

Over bare rocks
   the soft green moss;
Over deep wounds
   a healing balm:

Through stifling air
   a freshening breeze;
A lightning flash –
   the soul is freed.

(Given by Una Marson to Egon and Ursula Larsen in London, the original was passed to Erika Waters by the Larsens.)

MAY

Indeed you are well named –
Fickle young May
For what you will do
Who can say
Yesterday you were smiling
But today we see
You are frowning and dour
And with us disagree;
Tomorrow, who knows,
You may pour your tears
As though you'd never wept
Throughout the years.

Don't you think it's a shame
To behave like this,
When you start with gay revels
And the May Queen's kiss?
With fair cherry blossoms
Adorning your bowers
In your hair, on your lap
In your hands lovely flowers?
For shame, dry your tears
And smile to meet June
With eyes full of love
He's coming so soon.

(The page heading to this poem has Marson's Washington address
which indicates that the poem was written between 1952 and 1960
when she resident in the city.)

175

THE SEED

Walking along a quiet street
I heard what seemed to be
The rat tat tat of a machine gun,
It was not that loud
But still it was sharp and insistent.

I looked about and then upwards
And on the balcony of a high house
I saw a little boy of six or seven
Dressed in what looked like khaki
A white tin helmet on his head
Drawn low over his forehead.

He stood behind a perfect replica
Of a modern machine gun;
(Alas his parents must have given it him)
And there he was, his little face
Shining and glowing with delight
Dealing death to all who passed that way.

I felt cold and shivery as though
The pellets he sprayed were bullets
As though suddenly I knew hate and death
(Had I not lived through the last war)
And this came from the hands and heart
Of a little child of whom Christ said
"Of such is the Kingdom of Heaven"

For weeks this spectacle haunted me;
And even now, as I write
I hear the rattle and see the delight
On that child's face.
Can it be that parents don't know
That if you plant a seed it will grow.

THE JOY OF MOUNTAINS

Beautiful and close
To my heart
Are the mountains and hills
That rise from the plains
Of Kingston
To adorn St. Andrew
And mount
Heavenward.

Beautiful and pure
Are the drifting clouds
That float earthward
To love and caress you
As they fall asleep
In your arms
While soft pink rays
From the setting sun
Cast a magic spell
About you.

Grateful and blest
Are the eyes of my people
That can be lifted up
To behold this glory
Untouched and unspoilt
By the hand of man.
Praise be to Him
Who spreads before us
This banquet of joy
This feast of delight
To inspire and bless
Each hour
Of each day.

NOTES

"To Hampton", p. 61: Hampton High School was a private school
that catered for the middle-class daughters of Jamaican families
not quite wealthy enough to send their children to England.
Marson won a Free Foundationer's Scholarship and entered the
school as a border in 1915. She followed her sisters Edith and
Ethel, who had both excelled academically. Most of the pupils
were white and, despite the enthusiastic portrait of a busy and
contented life that this poem crafts, other accounts suggest that
she was very conscious of the racialised values that still operated.
A fuller account of Marson's time at Hampton is offered in the
short second chapter of Delia Jarrett-Macauley's biography *The
Life of Una Marson, 1905-1965* (Manchester University Press,
1998).

"To Wed or Not to Wed", p. 63: This poem was first published in
The Cosmopolitan in the August issue of 1929 (p. 137). Interest-
ingly, it appeared alongside a reprinted column from the London
Daily Mirror that debates the subject, 'Are Women Good Bosses?'.
This piece concludes that women are generally 'too easily
influenced by personal feeling. Not sufficiently detached intel-
lectually; either to reach an impassionate, unbiased judgement
about important matters; or to act quickly, effectively, and justly
in matters of daily routine'. The author, Walter Ashley, adopts
an exceedingly arrogant and patronising tone that is set into
wonderful relief by Marson's stringent and comic tone. Her
parody of Hamlet's agonising and existential soliloquy brings the
marriage question forward for amusing but insightful scrutiny.

"There Will Come a Time", p. 80: To my knowledge this is the one
occasion where Marson makes direct reference to her mixed
ancestry. Although her maternal great-grandfather was Irish,
Marson consistently chose not to play to this heritage, instead
claiming Africa as a source of pride and identity at a time when
the Eurocentric ideals of beauty and culture were championed

in middle class Jamaica. The idea of unity that drives the ethical momentum of this work clearly situates her own declaration of mixed 'blood' within a progressive framing of a future society in which equality, rather difference, becomes the primary condition of human relatedness.

"Education", p. 88: This poem is a parody of Brutus's soliloquy in Shakespeare's *Julius Caesar*, Act 2, scene 1. Brutus's searching for a motive to agree the assassination of Caesar when he has no personal grudge or justification is rehearsed here in order to expose the flawed and controversial logic that prevented access to education for black students on the grounds of possible, rather than actual, 'harm'.

"The Banjo Boy", p. 123: It was this poem that Marson read as her contribution to the American poetry programme of *Voice*, in November 1942. This BBC six-part poetry magazine was aimed at broadcasting lesser-known writings and yet it featured some towering figures. Both William Empson and George Orwell presented and read works by other poets. This rather timid and gauche poetic figuring of the banjo boy is an interesting choice given that she had published far bolder, more subtle and poetically accomplished works that sought to give subjectivity to black figures in *The Moth and the Star*, six years earlier.

"Winifred Holtby", p. 130. Best-known today as a novelist, Winifred Holtby was also an important pacifist and lectured for the League of Nations. She came to know Marson through their shared links with the British Commonwealth League. Holtby died in 1935 from sclerosis of the kidneys. In an article entitled, 'Winifred Holtby – As I Knew Her,' published on 5 June 1937, in the Jamaican weekly *Public Opinion* (p. 9), Marson discusses her interest in Holtby's 1933 novel *Mandoa, Mandoa* which is set in an imaginary African state. She explains how delighted she was to meet the author when they were both speakers at a conference of the British Commonwealth League in 1934 and how she 'saw a great deal of this enchanting woman who became more than an inspiration to me'. Indeed, it would seem that Holtby had supported Marson's writing and been a motivating force behind her narrative, *Autobiography of a Brown Girl*, that remains unpublished and in private hands. In this article, Marson records how, 'I never missed a conference or meeting at which she was speaking… She encouraged me to write a book of my experiences in Europe. She felt it would be a real contribution to the solution of the problem of racial antagonism and make for better understanding between races'.

"To the I.A.W.S.E.C.", p. 131: The International Alliance of Women for Suffrage and Equal Citizenship was founded in Washington, U.S., in 1902 by leading American suffragists. At the Congress of 1926 in Paris, the name International Women's Alliance was adopted.

In April 1935 Marson was asked to represent the Women's Social Service Club of Jamaica at the I.A.W.S.E.C.'s twelfth congress in Istanbul, Turkey. She was the first woman of African descent to present to the congress. The sonnet indicates how inspired and heartened Marson was by the solidarity and purposeful activity that she encountered. Accounts suggest that her own address, that drew strong attention to questions of racial discrimination, was received with great interest. The Alliance had strong links with the League of Nations and Marson was contacted by the League's Secretary and asked to act as a collaborator in their work. Again, she was the first woman of African descent to take on this role and travelled to Geneva in 1935, where she later offered her services to the Abyssinian Legation as the crisis with Italy unfolded.

"To Joe and Ben", p. 132: The Joe and Ben of this poem are Joseph and Benjamin Martin, the two sons of Dr Charles Martin, the Abyssinian minister in London, who were murdered by the Italians in 1937, after their capture in Wollega.

"At the Prison Gates", p. 136: This poem, broadcast on the BBC in September 1942, is reproduced in *Towards the Stars*, pp. 58-60. It was been lightly revised for the later publication. Although substantially the same, the 1945 version emphasises the poem as an act of historical record with the subtitle, Jamaica, 1937. The truncated ending also foregrounds the continuation of struggle as it concludes: 'Among those who rule the land/ In politics and those who rule in gold. /But the tramp of the weary feet still sound, / On they march –must they march on forever?'

"Cinema Eyes", p. 138: This poem by Marson is both exceptionally astute and pioneering in its critique of white cinema and the pressure this industry exerts on black women to conform to false icons of white beauty. This subject is also dealt with in 1940 in a letter to *The Keys*, the publication of the League of Coloured Peoples, that Marson edited for some years. Reviewing *Gone With the Wind*, Arthur Lewis, an economics professor at the University of Manchester, argues that film has made the black characters comic and underplayed the domestic power and knowledge that they showed in the novel (*Letter no 9*, June 1940, p. 50). Much more recently, Toni Morrison's novel, *The Bluest Eye* (1970), documents an obsession with cinema as a source of alienation and psychological harm. The young black protagonist of this novel, Pecola Breedlove, prays ardently every night to be transformed into a blue-eyed beauty like Shirley Temple.

"They Also Serve", p. 163: The title from this poem is taken from the closing line of John Milton's famous sonnet 'On His Blindness' that was often invoked during both World War I and II to refer to those who were not directly involved in battle. The poem appears, rather anomalously in 'Poems of Nature', set apart from the other poems that focus on wartime activities. This placement may be explained by the fact that this poem sits alongside another poem about the Isle on Man that Marson invokes in 'Farewell' by reference to Ellan Vannin, the Manx name for the Isle of Man (*Towards the Stars*, p. 19).

ABOUT THE AUTHOR

Una Marson was born in Jamaica in 1905, the daughter of a Baptist minister. She worked as the assistant editor of a Jamaican political journal and in 1928 launched her own magazine, *The Cosmopolitan*, which dealt with local, feminist and workers' rights issues, aimed at a progressive middle class audience. In 1930 she self-published her first collection of poems, *Tropic Reveries*, followed by *Heights and Depths* (1931), and her first play, *At What Price*. Between 1932-36, Marson went to England, and her poetry was marked by her confrontation with racism, and her feminism was deepened by the International Alliance of Women. Returning to Jamaica she worked as a journalist and wrote two further plays and a third collection of poetry. She went to London between 1938-1945, where her most important work with the BBC led to the creation of the hugely influential Caribbean Voices programme. She also became involved with the pan-Africanist anti-colonial movement in this period. Her life after 1945 is far from clear, but involved time in both Jamaica and the USA. In Jamaica she was one of the early defenders of the Rastafarian movement from persecution.

ABOUT THE EDITOR

Dr. Alison Donnell is a reader in the Department of English Language and Literature at the University of Reading. She is the author of *Twentieth Century Caribbean Literature: Critical Moments in Anglophone Literary and Critical History* (2006) and co-edited *The Routledge Reader in Caribbean Literature,* (1996), *Representing Lives, Women and Auto/biography* (2000) and *The Routledge Companion to Anglophone Caribbean Literature* (2011).

OTHER CARIBBEAN MODERN CLASSICS

Now in print:

Wayne Brown, *On The Coast*
ISBN 9781845231507, pp. 115, £8.99
Jan Carew, *Black Midas*
ISBN 9781845230951, pp.272 £8.99
Jan Carew, *The Wild Coast*
ISBN 9781845231101, pp. 240; £8.99
Austin Clarke, *Amongst Thistles and Thorns*
ISBN 9781845231477, pp.208; £8.99
Neville Dawes, *The Last Enchantment*
ISBN 9781845231170, pp. 332; £9.99
Wilson Harris, *Heartland*
ISBN 9781845230968, pp. 104; £7.99
George Lamming, *Of Age and Innocence*
ISBN 9781845231453, pp.438; £14.99
Earl Lovelace, *While Gods Are Falling*
ISBN 9781845231484, pp. 258; £10.99
Edgar Mittelholzer, *Corentyne Thunder*
ISBN 9781845231118, pp. 242; £8.99
Edgar Mittelholzer, *A Morning at the Office*
ISBN 9781845230661, pp.210; £9.99
Edgar Mittelholzer, *Shadows Move Among Them*
ISBN 9781845230913, pp. 358; £12.99
Edgar Mittelholzer, *The Life and Death of Sylvia*
ISBN 9781845231200, pp. 366; £12.99
Andrew Salkey, *Escape to an Autumn Pavement*
ISBN 9781845230982, pp. 220; £8.99
Denis Williams, *Other Leopards*
ISBN 9781845230678, pp. 216; £8.99
Denis Williams, *The Third Temptation*
ISBN 9781845231163, pp. 108; £8.99

George Campbell, *First Poems*

Austin C. Clarke, *The Survivors of the Crossing*

O.R. Dathorne, *The Scholar Man*

O.R. Dathorne, *Dumplings in the Soup*

Neville Dawes, *Interim*

Wilson Harris, *The Eye of the Scarecrow*

Wilson Harris, *The Sleepers of Roraima*

Wilson Harris, *Tumatumari*

Wilson Harris, *Ascent to Omai*

Wilson Harris, *The Age of the Rainmakers*

Marion Patrick Jones, *Panbeat*

Marion Patrick Jones, *Jouvert Morning*

George Lamming, *Water with Berries*

Roger Mais, *The Hills Were Joyful Together*

Roger Mais, *Black Lightning*

Edgar Mittelholzer, *Children of Kaywana*

Edgar Mittelholzer, *The Harrowing of Hubertus*

Edgar Mittelholzer, *Kaywana Blood*

Edgar Mittelholzer, *My Bones and My Flute*

Edgar Mittelholzer, *A Swarthy Boy*

Elma Napier, *A Flying Fish Whispered*

Orlando Patterson, *The Children of Sisyphus*

Orlando Patterson, *An Absence of Ruins*

V.S. Reid, *New Day*

V.S. Reid, *The Leopard* (North America only)

Garth St. Omer, *A Room on the Hill*

Garth St. Omer, *Shades of Grey*

Andrew Salkey, *The Late Emancipation of Jerry Stover*

and more…

All Peepal Tree titles are available from the website
www.peepaltreepress.com
with a money back guarantee, secure credit card ordering
and fast delivery throughout the world at cost or less.

Or contact us at:
Peepal Tree Press, 17 King's Avenue, Leeds LS6 1QS, UK
Tel: +44 (0) 113 2451703 E-mail: contact@peepaltreepress.com